THE CATALOG HANDBOOK

The
CATALOG
HANDBOOK

How to Produce a Successful Mail Order Catalog

JAMES FRANCIS HOLLAN III

HIPPOCRENE BOOKS, INC.
New York

Special thanks to Terry Griest for teaching me most of what I know about retailing; Larry Vincent, Joyce Kaminkow and Terry Drake for reading and advising; Typography Two for information and jokes; Mr. Bernie Grayson (R.I.P.), a great cat, for making me smile; and Louise Moore for reading and advising, but most of all for keeping my feet on the ground—no easy task!

ISBN 0-87052-071-7

For information, address:
HIPPOCRENE BOOKS, INC.
171 Madison Ave.
New York, NY 10016

Library of Congress Cataloging-in-Publication Data is available.

Printed in the United States of America.

Dedicated to My Father,
James Francis Hollan

CONTENTS

	Introduction	9
CHAPTER ONE	Why Would Someone Buy From You?	11
CHAPTER TWO	Your Catalog Design	17
CHAPTER THREE	Your First Rough	27
CHAPTER FOUR	The Front Cover	37
CHAPTER FIVE	The Back Cover	53
CHAPTER SIX	The Order Form	57
CHAPTER SEVEN	Art and Photography	65
CHAPTER EIGHT	Copy	71
CHAPTER NINE	Your Second Rough	75
CHAPTER TEN	Printers	87
CHAPTER ELEVEN	Mail Lists and Mailing	93
CHAPTER TWELVE	Your Final Rough	103
CHAPTER THIRTEEN	The Paste-Up	109
CHAPTER FOURTEEN	How Much Does It Cost?	115
CHAPTER FIFTEEN	Increasing Profits	121
CHAPTER SIXTEEN	Evaluating Your Catalog	135
	Sources and Resources	139
	Index	144

Introduction

This is a "how-to" book about the mail order business with a special emphasis on producing a good but inexpensive first catalog. In this business, like anything else in life, the more work you do yourself, the more money you will save. In fact you can save a fortune by using common sense and knowing what key mistakes not to make.

The production of a catalog is not very difficult. I assume that if you are reading this book you are at least vaguely interested in the topic and you have an idea for a catalog floating around in the back of your head somewhere. More than likely you would like to know what it takes to put a catalog together. What does it cost? How do you do it? Where do you get all those names for a mailing? How do you get started?

In 1981, my partner and I literally sat down at our kitchen table and drafted our first catalog. We wrote the articles and product descriptions. We took the photos or drafted ideas for the drawings we would need. We chose the layouts and type styles. We did much of the paste-up ourselves and we went door to door comparing printers until we found how to get the most for the least investment. Although we had very little money to invest, we had boundless energy and we were willing to take some risks.

That first catalog was black and white, printed on the cheapest quality of newsprint. In fact, we copied the layout from an old high school newspaper. It was amateurish and riddled with mistakes but it put us in the mail order business and we made a profit on our very first mailing. Maybe we were on the bottom rung of the mail order ladder but at least we were on the ladder and the only place to go was up.

Our products were unique. We featured a wide assortment of goods from Scotland and Ireland. We made a point of stocking hard-to-locate items for the piper or dancer. We had swords and bagpipes and kilts for men. We had handmade sweaters and skirts in family tartans for women. We made our uniqueness work for us and we slowly grew from mailing a few thousand black and white catalogs produced at home into a multimillion dollar mail order business producing full-color catalogs advertised nationwide in the *New York Times* and *Smithsonian Magazine*. We were featured in worldwide ads for AT&T and our customer list included Malcom Forbes and the White House.

Along the way I've made most every mistake at least once but I've learned from those mistakes. Whenever I give a talk about mail order I'm constantly asked for a practical introduction to the field. I get calls on a regular basis from people wanting to start a small catalog. They want a basic guide to follow. They want to know the secrets of the trade.

The mail order industry is becoming more sophisticated and more expensive to enter. Many companies commit millions of dollars to their first catalog venture. If you have that kind of money this book is not for you. Go out and hire a top agency and it will give you the catalog of your dreams. You'll love it!

I've written this book for the small business that has limited capital and must make every dollar work like ten. It's written for the individual who wants to explore the possibility of mail order without investing a fortune. I've used real dollar figures so you can get a rough estimate of costs. I've included my mistakes so you may avoid them and stressed those things that were successful so you can copy them. I've tried to be honest so that you can see what you are in for.

As the large catalogs become larger, I believe more and more room will be created for small specialized catalogs. I believe people are getting tired of homogenized America and are more and more interested in those things they don't see in every mall. I believe a good idea can still sell and I believe mail order is the way to reach the broadest group of potential buyers. I've written this book for all the people out there with something they want to market. If a guy in Annapolis can make a fortune selling bagpipes by mail, can your idea really be so crazy?

CHAPTER ONE

Why Would Someone Buy From You?

Well, why would someone buy from you? Is your product better than the others? Is it cheaper? Is it unique? Do you see a special part of the market nobody else seems to see? Do you have something out of the ordinary?

You must have a good reason for someone to buy from you. No matter how pretty your catalog is, no one is going to buy from you if you're charging twice as much as everyone else. I am constantly amazed at the number of catalogs that hit the market then quickly disappear because they look just like all the others and advertise the same products at similar prices. If you are a general gift store selling the same sort of merchandise found in most mall stores at about the same price, let me save you a lot of money and heartache—DON'T GO INTO MAIL ORDER.

In the last few years it seems every other magazine has had an article about the fortunes to be made in mail order. Even *Time* magazine featured a catalog on its cover. Sometimes it seems like everyone in Western civilization has jumped into the mail order business. Our mailboxes are filled with catalogs. It is a highly competitive field. If you don't know what you're doing you can lose a bundle fast.

Here is a simple drill that you should find useful. Assume you are going to set up a catalog. At first you can answer the questions in your head, and you probably won't know all the answers in the beginning. But over time your answers should get more and more detailed and your ideas more precise.

Preliminary Questionnaire

1) *Are there any catalogs like yours on the market?* If you answer "yes," you should get those catalogs and examine them closely. *What do they do well? What do they do badly? How would you improve on them? What are their weak points? Can you exploit those weak points? Do they have strengths you might find hard to match? If a customer received your catalog and theirs on the same day, why would he buy from you and not them?* If you are uncertain, why? *Is your idea so new that no one has tried it?* Maybe you have found a real niche in the market that is too small for the big boys to fool with, but you may also be beating your head against a brick wall.

2) *Who is your customer? Mostly men? Older? Younger? Working class? Yuppies? Highly educated? Vain? Parents? Christians? New Age? Surfers as opposed to golfers?* Obviously anyone can buy from you but you probably are considering special segments of the market. *What will you emphasize?*

3) *What products will you sell? Can you get sufficient supplies of an item if it sells a lot? Do you have a number of good items or just one or two winners? Can you stock a lot of these items? If you run out can you restock quickly?*

4) *What theme holds your products together? All made in France? All for left-handed people? All for well dressed men? For professional women? For history buffs? For ex-hippies?*

These questions may seem basic to you but I've been amazed at the number of people who haven't really considered them. Don't even think about going into mail order if you don't know the answers. Why? Because those answers will be the foundation of your first catalog. You may not have all the right answers and you will definitely change some answers over time but you must begin somewhere.

Let me illustrate by going back to 1981 and our first catalog. Our store had a theme, Scottish and Irish imports. We sold all sorts of items from these two countries and we felt we had an interesting niche in the market. We wanted to expand and felt mail order was a real possibility so we answered these questions in the following way:

1) *Were there any catalogs like ours in the market?* Yes. We got these catalogs and tried to be as objective as possible in our evaluation of each. (We ordered two by phone and clipped ads for the others—a total investment of $5 to see what our main competition was doing). Here is an abbreviated version of our evaluation:

SHANNON MAIL ORDER—A full color catalog offering goods mostly from Ireland with some items from other parts of the world. Very large selection of crystal and china. Although an Irish catalog, it does not create any sense of Ireland. The paper and layout is fair. General sense of quality is fair. Prices are very good—in some cases terrific. Prices are duty free. Only two pages of sweaters, throws and clothing. Almost no gift items besides crystal and china and very little jewelry. The strength of this catalog is its duty free prices, its association with Shannon Airport, and its great selection of Waterford crystal. The main weakness is the confusing and difficult order process and we believe many people are nervous sending money overseas.

SCOTTISH LION—This is a very attractive full color catalog from North Conway, New Hampshire. It is the most professional of the competitive catalogs. They are very strong in clothing and upper end jewelry. They do a great job of showing a very large selection of tartans in color. We can't beat the look of this book. They are expensive and I think we can beat them on price; moreover, they do very little of the hard core ethnic goods that we feature and stock. They do very little Irish and almost no books or records.

OTHER—There are two or three small catalogs that have very little impact on the market or are very difficult to acquire. The best of the lot is one out of Chicago called Maggies Irish Imports. It is all Irish, black & white, but tastefully done. It has a more conventional Irish gift shop selection and prices are somewhat higher than ours. They feature some items we have seen but chosen not to buy because of different taste, different market.

On the bottom of the pile of other catalogs are a few mimeographed sheets of record or book titles that really aren't catalogs for general buyers.

2) *Why would people buy from us and not the others?* There were several reasons. We offer a number of items the others don't. We have a better selection on some items. We have better prices on some items. We believe we have a different image to present by combining Scottish and Irish to hit both markets. We cater to the hard core ethnic hobbyist.

3) *Who is our customer?* Obviously we want to sell to everyone but we have a few different types.

HARD CORE ETHNIC BUYER—mostly men, mostly middle aged, members of Scottish societies such as St. Andrew's or Robert Burns, and Irish societies such as Hibernians and Friendly Sons of St. Patrick.

GENEALOGICAL BUYER—no age or sex emphasis here. People interested in their roots, family history; however, they are usually not scholars and don't want to spend a lot of money.

FOLKIES—younger, not a lot of money, like fun "different" things. Aren't especially Scottish or Irish.

PSEUDO-ETHNIC BUYER—wants a gift that says Ireland or Scotland out loud. Usually not very well informed, wants instant heritage, will spend a little to a moderate amount of money.

4) *What products will we sell?* After reviewing the other catalogs we would be smart not to emphasize crystal and china since it is done with a better selection and at cheaper prices than we can hope for. We would also be wise to play down fashion since we can only afford black and white and it is hard to sell fashion without showing the rich colors. It doesn't make a lot of sense to say this $195 sweater is sort of purplish with little flecks of brown stuff!

We will fill the gaps with goods that our competitors are not pushing. These include records, books, music, bagpipes and bagpipe supplies, flags, and heraldic items. We will push highland attire and equipment and we will heavily advertise our special order and custom made products.

We will compete with some items others have because they are good sellers for us in the store and we either have a better price or just don't feel like backing off. For example we charge more for an Aran sweater than Shannon Mail Order, however, we feel many people may not get

Shannon's catalog or they may be nervous about ordering overseas or having to pay duty.

We cannot show top line items very well in black and white; therefore, we will emphasize this apparent weakness and stress our folksy homemade quality and our prices.

That is a very rough outline of the way we answered the basic questions. We assumed when we started that if an item sold well we could get more of it. This was a stupid and naive assumption. Murphy's Law seems to state that your suppliers will always be out of your best sellers. We will deal with the problems of stock and supplier agreements later in this book. For now I want to explain how we came up with a preliminary outline of what we wanted to do.

Before we did any work on our catalog we developed a rough customer profile. Then we had to decide how to reach that type of customer with our limited resources. We would change our mind about many things later but this was our starting point. We had a direction for our catalog and you must have one also.

Take the time to consider your answers to the above questions. In the beginning just make your best guess. There is no one right answer. This is not a science. Business is an art. Don't be overly optimistic or overly pessimistic. Do try to be fair. It is tempting to see only the flaws in a competitor's catalog because you hate the competitor. You must see his strengths if you hope to overcome them.

When you have a customer profile you can better direct your catalog at that customer. If you think your customer will be older than average you may plan to use larger type and feature a more conventional layout, whereas a younger crowd might respond better to an unconventional approach. Before you go anywhere you must have some sense of who you are trying to reach.

CHAPTER TWO

Your Catalog Design

Steal From the Best—Leave Out the Rest

You are not going to reinvent the wheel! Thousands of catalogs are out there designed by people who are experts. The contents may be very different but the designs are remarkably similar. Some are bigger, some are smaller, some are beautiful, and some are ugly, but they all clearly tell you, "We are a catalog." They are not usually confused with novels or with cookbooks. You glance at certain collections of papers and know in an instant you are looking at a catalog. Why?

The first thing to do about your catalog design is to see what everyone else is doing and learn from experience. You need to look at catalogs in a different way now. You probably have been looking at them as a customer. You will now look at them as a catalog builder.

Over the years companies have paid millions of dollars to designers, graphic artists, psychologists and marketing experts in order to produce better and more effective catalogs. All of that information is free to you if you are willing to look at it. It's a gift. These strangers are going to save you a fortune. Let me show you how to focus on this wealth of information.

The first thing to do is build a large collection of catalogs. You are probably receiving a bunch already. If not, you can ask friends and relatives to save all the catalogs they get for the next week or two. Since you are serious about the catalog business you should be getting on mailing lists by now anyway.

The catalogs don't have to be current. They can be a year or so old. Even though we are talking about starting a black and white catalog, you should collect color catalogs also. In fact the vast majority of catalogs these days are in color and the bulk of your pile should be color.

You do not want to collect the advertising flyers that are inserted in newspapers. In particular, the color sections from department stores usually found in a Sunday paper are not really catalogs, although they often have a similar appearance. They do not encourage mail order sales; rather, they direct you to a store.

Try to get a good cross section of catalogs so that you have some high quality flashy catalogs as well as some cheap and tacky ones. You want to look at the entire spectrum. In fact you should have at least 50 or 60 catalogs in your pile before you go to the next step. At this stage a bad catalog can also be very instructive. Let me now introduce you to the designer's best friend, the clip file.

What is a clip file? It is a professional name for the place you keep all your stolen ideas. No self respecting designer would be caught without a drawer full of them. You need about eight or ten file folders. The cheap cardboard kind that are about 9″ × 12″ work fine. You can find these at any stationery store or the school supply section of most drugstores. You will also need a marker and a pair of scissors.

Label one of the folders "Front Covers" and another "Back Covers." Now with scissors in hand, go through your pile of catalogs and cut off the covers so that you have 30 examples of each in the proper folder. Later in this book we will deal with catalog covers and you will pull out the appropriate file of examples. You will be able to compare the effect of different type styles and how others display the company name. What kind of art did they use? Can you do something similar? Can you see a way to do it better? Cheaper?

A clip art file is a gold mine of helpful information as you approach each catalog element. For the moment you will organize your basic clip files so you can use them with the appropriate chapters later in this book. Notice that we do not use all the catalogs in our pile for our clip files. As important as it is to look at elements of a catalog in detail, it is also important to look at a catalog as a whole; therefore, you will also keep a collection of unclipped catalogs for later use.

Make another file labeled "Order Forms." Most order forms do not need to be cut out as they are stapled into the catalog. You want to put 30 or so of these in your clip file. So far it's sort of fun, isn't it?

Everyone needs a clip file for the first three elements. You now start to specialize a bit based on your specific needs. If you are going to sell lots of food items and cooking utensils you might clip displays featuring arrangements of these products and label the clip file "food/gourmet." For my catalog I had a clip file for each of these areas: books, records, clothing, music, small gifts, and jewelry.

In addition to these clip files and the three for covers and order forms, I also kept one other file that wasn't really a clip art file. I labeled this file "Good Ideas" and used it for various odd bits I might see in catalogs. These might be a cute way of featuring a sale or an especially interesting layout I might be able to copy. If a good idea caught my eye, it got clipped and went into this folder.

As you assemble your clip files you should not try to be too critical. If something is vaguely interesting, file it now. You can always throw it out later. You want to sort and collect information so that it is immediately on hand when you are ready for it. As you see, the process is not very difficult; moreover, you do not outgrow it. You should always be watching for good ideas. When you see them you should clip and file them.

We will use your clip files later in this book, but for now let's go back to the pile of unclipped catalogs and start flipping pages. You should start looking at page layouts, the way pages are organized.

Each page has two key elements, copy and art. The words are the copy and the drawings or photos are the art. On occasion a page may be only one or the other but in general a page has both of these elements. In its simplest form, *layout* is the way you arrange the art and copy on a page.

Some catalogs emphasize art. They are very big on photography and don't need a lot of words if the photos do what they are supposed to do. This is often a legitimate approach when marketing high fashion or jewelry.

Other catalogs emphasize copy. In particular you see this emphasis

in technical or special interest catalogs, such as those featuring electronics, where the potential customer wants to know all sorts of specific details about the featured products. Many specialized book catalogs use very little art, perhaps a few illustrations at best.

Art costs more than copy. You must pay for the drawings or photos.
You may be paying for models and hair stylists. You may need to rent a
studio or pay professional photographers and artists. You must pay for
screening or separating color art in order to prepare it for printing. You
need better quality papers for better quality reproduction. The costs
mount quickly; nevertheless, you won't get very far with a catalog that
uses no art. People expect art in a catalog and you better deliver. You
want to maximize the impact of art while minimizing its cost.

As you flip the pages in your pile of unclipped catalogs you should
start noticing how others are using art and copy. Start noticing things
like where the descriptions are placed relative to the art. Is it clear what
goes with what or is it confusing? How would you improve it? Look for
very symmetrical layouts. How do they appear to you? Boring? Interesting? Compare them with asymmetrical layouts. Which do you prefer? You will probably start to notice that most catalogs have a certain
pattern within the catalog, so that a similar layout is used throughout.
You are not looking at covers or order forms at this stage, just the
catalog pages.

Let's look more closely at the types of layouts you've seen. As we do
this you should keep asking yourself how these ideas may apply to
your catalog plans. Would your products fit better into one format or
the other? Do you have a lot of options or very few? You don't need to
decide anything yet but you should be developing a better understanding of what is already out there and be starting to get a sense of
how it may work for you.

Let's take a page from one of my early catalogs and see how I
approached a layout for books (Example 1). I used a perfectly symmetrical grid that is boring but effective. The catalog contained three
pages of books, all laid out the same. A photo of the cover was placed
in each box with the code, copy and price below each. The top center
graphic was lifted from a book of free advertising art.

The layout is about as basic and primitive as you can get. We were
able to show 18 titles per page and for an early effort this page was

EXAMPLE 1

Books

48184 I AM OF IRELAND — A delightful colour photo essay capturing the faces of Ireland, 64 pages **$6.95**

48982 AN IRISH BLESSING — Colour photo essay using an Irish Blessing as its theme. Makes a lovely gift, 64 pages **$6.95**

4014343 GHOSTS IN IRISH HOUSES — Strange tales of ghosts and the supernatural with illustrations by the author, James Reynolds **$7.95**

4094302 BRACE YOURSELF BRIGIT — This Irish "SEX MANUAL" makes a delightful gift as all the pages are blank, write your own **$5.95**

4436017 IRISH EROTIC ART — Another comic cover for a blank page book. Draw your own pictures **$5.95**

436238 IRISH SHOP FRONTS — Wonderful colour collection of shops & shop fronts from all over Ireland . . . . '**7.95**

4145189 CONCISE HISTORY OF IRELAND — An impartial history from Elizabethan times to the troubles in Belfast, 174 illustrations **$5.95**

48109 THE IRISH WORLD — Over 340 illustrations, including 62 full colour plates unites the whole of Irish history in this oversize book. **$40.00**

SPECIAL

48400 HISTORY OF IRISH FLAGS — 240 pages packed with photos tracing the history of Irish flags and banners. Orig. $45.00, ... **$19.95**

4379899 STORY OF THE IRISH PEOPLE — Sean O'Faolains study of what social changes made the Irish what they are **$3.95**

4064081 STORY OF IRISH RACE — New revised edition of the Seamus MacManus saga of Irish history & culture, 700 pages **$6.95**

423796 CELTIC DESIGN COLORING BOOK — Filled with large drawings of Celtic designs ready for you to colour. **$2.00**

47396 BOOK OF KELLS — First rate study of this Irish masterpiece profusely illustrated in full colour **$10.95**

48255 LION OF IRELAND — Best selling novel that brings to life the Legend of Brian Boru, the first High King of Ireland **$3.50**

4129582 ART OF IRISH COOKING — Traditional Irish recipes by Monica Sheridan presented with wit and flair . . . . '**2.95**

4276704 IRISH COOKING — Authentic, easy to prepare dishes from the Emerald Isles with nearly 30 full colour photos **$3.95**

4127318 500 BEST IRISH JOKES — A super collection of one liners, groaners and shaggy dog stories **$2.95**

402158 BOOK OF BLARNEY — Butler's hilarious study of Irish blarney and how to blarney back **$2.95**

effective. Most importantly all three book pages were highly profitable.

If you examine Examples 2 and 3 you will see how I treated records in the same early catalog. The two pages faced each other. The first thing you will probably notice is that I used three columns instead of the four used for books. I much prefer the look of three on a page. It appears less cluttered. We were able to show a lot of product because titles could be collected under subheads making less description necessary for each unit. Because of this I was able to display 34 titles on one page and 31 on the other, just about double the number of book titles in the same space.

We chose not to illustrate every title; therefore, I was able to use larger photos of those titles I did feature. You should take a minute and examine all three pages. They are simple solutions to basic problems. Looking back I must say that I think the record layout is far superior to the book layout. Not only is it more pleasing visually but it also sells more product. A weakness I did not see at the time, but customers were nice enough to point out in letters, is that the type was too small and very difficult to read for my older customers. I did not realize that I would attract as many older buyers as I ultimately did.

After customers complained about difficulty reading the catalog, I changed to the format shown in Example 4. In order to accommodate the larger type size I moved to a two-column layout. If you look carefully you will see that I also changed the copy style. In the first examples I used a code number, the title in bold and then the price. I switched to the title in bold, a description, the code and the price. I think this is a more sensible format and easier to read.

In the next catalog we took the same two-column layout and made it a little more interesting (Example 5). As you can see, each change is a variation on its predecessor. Each layout is a combination of copy and art determined by our budget, our desire to show a lot of product in a limited space and our response to our customers. You can also see that complete amateurs were able to meet these challenges.

Later in this book we will deal with more involved and sophisticated layouts but the purpose of this chapter is to develop your focus. You now see how to collect and sort the various elements of your catalog. The next few chapters will show you how to sharpen that focus even more.

EXAMPLE 2

Records *FOR THE COLLECTOR*

BAG PIPES

We are pleased to announce that we are U.S. agents for Lismor Records, thereby holding stocks of the finest Scottish music. We welcome wholesale inquiries from legitimate dealers.

05111* Shotts & Dykehead Caledonia Pipe Band "CHAMPION OF CHAMPIONS" — Winners of 10 world championships $7.95
05009 Shotts & Dykehead Caledonia Pipe Band "SHORES OF LOCH KATRINE" $7.95
05038* Shotts & Dykehead Caledonia Pipe Band "THE CALEDONIA PIPE BAND" $7.95

05019 Dysart & Doundonald Pipe Band "SUPREME CHAMPIONS" — It seems when Shotts & Dykehead wasn't winning something, this band was $7.95
05051* Dysart & Dundonald Pipe Band "SKIRL OF THE BAGPIPES" . . . $7.95
05090* Dysart & Dundonald Pipe Band "World Champions" $7.95
01301 "PIPES & DRUMS OF THE ROYAL TANK REGIMENT" — Along with Cambrai Staff Band $6.95
02037 Invergordon Distillery Pipe Band — "PIPES IN CONCERT" $8.95
02004* The Scots Guards "SCOTS GUARDS IN CONCERT" $8.95
02038 The Scots Guards "SALUTE TO PAGENTRY" — with Pipe & Brass Band $7.95
022401 "WORLD PIPE CHAMPIONSHIPS 1980" includes Shotts & Dykehead, Strathclyde Police, Lothian & Boarders & others $10.95
Q966689 City Of Glasgow Police Pipe Band "SCOTTISH PIPE BAND MUSIC" $4.95

05041* Seumas MacNeill — "PURELY PIOBAIREACHD" $7.95
05089* Donald Macleod — "POSITIVELY PIOBAIREACHD" $7.95
043865 Seumans MacNeill — "THE HIGHLAND BAGPIPES" $4.95
092899 "EDINBURGH MILITARY TATOO" — Military bands, pipes, drums $4.95

FIDDLE

03430 John Turner — "MONTGOMERY BLUE" — Five time national Scottish Fiddle Champion. This album is mostly melodic "parlor" music. $8.95
03621 John Turner — "SCOTTISH MENAGERIE" — Fiddle, pipes, drums, voices — wonderful collection $8.95
02580 John Turner — "FIDDLING ROGUES & RASCALS VOL. 1" — John & friends — voices and other instruments $8.95
09405 John Turner — "FIDDLING ROGUES & RASCALS VOL. II" — More of the former $8.95
06549 John Turner — "STALKING THE WILD BAGPIPE" $8.95
05017* Ron Gonnella — "FIDDLERS FANCY" A Scottish master $7.95
05070* Ron Gonnella — "BURNS NIGHT" $7.95
05060* Glasgow Caledonian Strathspey & Reel Society "FIDDLES GALORE" $7.95

RECORDS — All of our records are 33⅓ albums. Those albums listed with a star (*) are also available as cassettes for the same price as the album. Sorry, no 8-track available.

SCOTTISH DANCE

05072* Donald MacLeod — "PIPE TUNES FOR HIGHLAND DANCING" $7.95
05097 Ian Holmes & His Scottish Band — "LET'S DANCE IN STRICT TEMPO" $7.95
05112* Lothian Scottish Dance Band — "IN STRICT TEMPO" $7.95

SILLY WIZARD

An excellent new Scottish folk group. They have everyone's feet tapping here.
079015 Silly Wizard — "CALEDONIAS HARDY SONS" $9.95
079016 Silly Wizard — "SO MANY PARTINGS" $9.95
079028 Silly Wizard — "WILD AND BEAUTIFUL" $9.95

SCOTLAND VARIOUS

05076* David Solley — "GREAT SONGS OF SCOTLAND" $7.95
05027* The Tartan Lads — "BY THE LOCHSIDE" $7.95
05049 The Tartan Lads — "SCOTLAND YET" $7.95
06003* Peter Morrison — "SON OF THE HOMELAND" $8.95

EXAMPLE 3

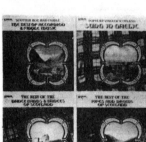

Great New Releases

05114 "THE BEST OF THE PIPES AND DRUMS OF SCOTLAND .. $7.95

05115 "THE BEST OF ACCORDIAN & FIDDLE MUSIC $7.95

05116 "THE BEST OF THE DANCE BANDS OF SCOTLAND $7.95

05117 "POPULAR SONGS OF SCOTLAND SUNG IN GAELIC . $7.95

SCOTLAND VARIOUS

05113" "TREASURES OF SCOTLAND" — Various artists including Peter Morrison, The Drifterfolk, David Solley, Ron Gonnella and The Tartan Lads in a tribute to the National Trust for Scotland $7.95
05075 Callum MacLean. — "SCOTTISH ACCORDIAN HITS VOL. 2" $7.95
05092" "ROBERT BURNS SONGBOOK" — Various artists performing the songs of Burns $7.95
05103" "HIGHLAND MAGIC" — Various artist perform Scottish tunes $7.95

05100 "ALL THE BEST FROM SCOTLAND" — Various artists including Stuart Anderson, Lomond Folk, David Solley, The Clydesiders, lots of songs and dance tunes $7.95

PLANXTY

Traditional Irish, superb instrumentals, earthy vocals, foot tapping, humorous . . .
079010 Planxty — "THE WELL BELOW THE VALLEY" — Christy Moore, Andy Irvine, Donald Lunny and Liam O'Flynn on Uileann- Pipes — A masterful album $9.95
079009 Planxty — "PLANXTY" $9.95
079011 Planxty — "COLD BLOW AND THE RAINY NIGHT" $9.95
079012 Planxty — "THE PLANXTY COLLECTION" $9.95
003001 Planxty — "AFTER THE BREAK" Recent album $10.95

DOLORES KEANE

03003 Dolores Keane — "FAREWELL TO ERIN" — Her latest album .. $9.95
03004 Dolores Keane — "BROKEN HEARTED I'LL WANDER" — My personal favorite $9.95

CLANCYS

000301 "BEST OF THE CLANCY BROS. & TOMMY MAKEN" — 3 record set $10.95
035609 "HEARTY IRISH FOLK SONGS" — Clancy Bros. & Tommy Makem $4.95
035633 "IRISH SONGS OF REBELLION" — Clancy Bros. & Tommy Makem $4.95
035595 "SONGS OF DRINKING AND BLACKGAURDING" Clancy Bros. & Tommy Makem $4.95
038403 "IRISH FOLK AIRS" — Clancy Bros. & their families $4.95

052004 "TWO FOR THE EARLY MORNING DEW" — Makem & Clancy $9.95
052001 "THE MAKEM & CLANCY COLLECTION" The best of their new tunes from recent concert tours ... $9.95

CHIEFTAINS

From Carnegie Hall in New York to Royal Albert Hall in London, the Chieftains are hailed worldwide as the greatest exponents of traditional Irish music.
079022 "CHIEFTAINS 2" $9.95
079023 "CHIEFTAINS 3" $9.95
079025 "CHIEFTAINS 5" $9.95
079026 "BONAPARTES RETREAT $9.95
079019 COTTON EYED JOE ... $9.95

HARP

079020 Derek Bell — "CAROLAN'S FAVORITE" — Derek is backed by the Chieftains and the New Irish Chamber Orchestra — superb album $9.95
079013 Derek Bell — "CAROLAN'S RECEIPT" $9.95
079014 Charles Guard — "AVENGING AND BRIGHT" — Great Irish harpist $9.95

PAGE 37

EXAMPLE 4

❧ Records for the Collector ☙

BAGPIPES

BEST OF THE PIPES AND DRUMS OF SCOTLAND — This is a superior collection of top quality bands.
05114* $7.95

CHAMPION OF CHAMPIONS — Shotts and Dykehead Pipe Band, winners of 10 World Championships.
05111* $7.95

SHORES OF LOCH KATRINE — Shotts and Dykehead Pipe Band.
05009 . . . . $7.95

THE CALEDONIA PIPE BAND — Shotts and Dykehead Pipe Band.
05038* $7.95

SUPREME CHAMPIONS — Dysart & Dundonald Pipe Band.
05019 . . . . $7.95

SKIRL OF THE BAGPIPES — Dysart & Dundonald Pipe Band.
05051* $7.95

WORLD CHAMPIONS — Dysart & Dundonald Pipe Band.
05090* $7.95

PIPES & DRUMS OF THE ROYAL TANK REGIMENT — Along with Cambrai Staff Band.
01301 . . . . $7.95

PIPES IN CONCERT — Invergordon Distillery Pipe Band.
02037 . . . . $8.95

SCOTS GUARDS IN CONCERT — Guards Pipe & Drum Band.
02004 . . . . $8.95

SALUTE TO PAGENTRY — Scots Guards with Pipe & Brass Band.
02038 . . . . $8.95

WORLD PIPE CHAMPIONSHIPS 1980 — Top bands include Shotts, Strathclyde Police, Lothian & Boarders and others.
022401 . . . . $10.95

SCOTTISH PIPE BAND MUSIC — Glasgow Police Pipe Band, an older album.
0966689 . . . . $4.95

THE HIGHLAND BAGPIPES — Seumas MacNeill, another older album.
043865 . . . . $4.95

PURELY PIOBAIREACHD — Seumas MacNeill, solo classical pipe music.
05041* $7.95

POSITIVELY PIOBAIREACHD —Donald MacLeod, another classic solo album.
05089* $7.95

CASSETTES
All albums with a star following their code number are also available as cassettes for the same price as the listed album.

FIDDLE

MONTGOMERY BLUE — John Turner, five time National Scottish Fiddle Champion. This album is mostly melodic "parlor" music.
03430 . . . . $9.95

THE GRACEFUL YOUNG WOMAN — Lovely new album by John Turner dedicated to his late wife.
07131 . . . . $9.95

THE SCOTTISH FIDDLERS OF LOS ANGELES — New collection by John Turner.
01386 . . . . $9.95

MUSICAL MENAGERIE — John Turner on fiddle accompanied by pipes, drums and voices.
03621 . . . . $9.95

BURNS NIGHT — Delightful collection of tunes played by Ron Gonnella.
05070* $7.95

FIDDLERS FANCY — Many violin favorites by Ron Gonnella.
05017* $7.95

FIDDLES GALORE — Glasgow Caledonian Strathspey & Reel Society.
05060 . . . . $7.95

SCOTLAND GENERAL

PIPE TUNES FOR HIGHLAND DANCING — Donald MacLeod collection for dancers and listeners.
05072* $7.95

LET'S DANCE IN STRICT TEMPO — Excellent for country dancers.
05097 . . . . $7.95

IN STRICT TEMPO — Lothian Scottish Dance Band.
05112* $7.95

CALEDONIAS HARDY SONS — Scottish folk songs by an exciting new group called Silly Wizard.
079015 . . . . $9.95

SO MANY PARTINGS — More folk tunes by Silly Wizard.
079016 . . . . $9.95

WILD & BEAUTIFUL — Most recent album by Silly Wizard.
079028 . . . . $9.95

POPULAR SONGS SUNG IN GAELIC — Good way to learn the language.
05117* $7.95

BEST DANCE BANDS OF SCOTLAND — Great sampler album.
05116* $7.95

BEST ACCORDIAN & FIDDLE OF SCOTLAND — A real toe tapper.
05115* $7.95

EXAMPLE 5

❦ RECORDS FOR THE COLLECTOR ❧

RIGHT OF THE LINE
The Pipes and Drums of the 1st Battallion of The Royal Scots. An excellent piping album.
025* $10.95

THE STRATHCLYDE POLICE PIPE BAND
World Champions, formerly the City of Glasgow Police Pipe Band.
05129* $7.95

PIPING FROM THE NORTH!
Music from the north of Scotland, the 1st album by the Turriff and District Pipe Band.
01* $10.95

MULL OF KINTYRE
A unique blend of popular, modern and traditional pipe music from the Campbeltown Pipe Band.
02* $8.95

THE MAGIC SOUNDS OF THE PIPES
Strathclyde Police, Dysart & Dundonald, Gordon Highlanders and other top bands.
08* $8.95

300 YEARS OF THE ROYAL SCOTS
300th anniversary album of Scotland's senior regiment.
040* $8.95

BAGPIPES

THE BEST OF THE PIPES AND DRUMS OF SCOTLAND
Our most popular collection of top quality bands.
05114* $7.95

CHAMPION OF CHAMPIONS
Shotts and Dykehead Pipe Band, winners of 10 World Championships.
05111* $7.95

THE CALEDONIA PIPE BAND
Shotts and Dykehead Pipe Band, current European champions.
)5038* $7.95

SUPREME CHAMPIONS
Dysart and Dundonald Pipe Band.
05019* $7.95

WORLD CHAMPIONS
Dysart and Dundonald Pipe Band.
05090* $7.95

SKIRL O' THE PIPES
Dysart and Dundonald Pipe Band.
05051* $7.95

WORLD PIPE CHAMPIONSHIPS 1980
Top bands including Shotts and Dykehead, Lothian and Boarders, Strathclyde Police and others.
022401 .... $10.95

EDINBURGH TATTOO 1982
Such groups as The Royal Scots, Gordon Highlanders, and the Queen's Own Highlanders. Was $9.95.
030* .... Now $5.95

EDINBURGH TATTOO 1983
Recorded live from the Castle Esplanade.
058* $9.95

SCOTS GUARD IN CONCERT
The Scots Guard Pipes and Drums, known the world over.
02004* $8.95

SCOTTISH PIPE BAND MUSIC
Glasgow Police Pipe Band, an older album.
0966689 .... $4.95

MILITARY BANDS, PIPES AND DRUMS OF SCOTLAND
A 5 record set including Amazing Grace and Scotland the Brave.
0955393 .... $14.95

ANNIVERSARY BOUQUET - THE CAMBRAI STAFF BAND
A "bouquet" of old favourites and new original compositions.
01301 .... $7.95

THE HIGHLAND BAGPIPES
Pipe tunes by Donald MacPherson
043865 .... $4.95

PIPE MAJOR JOHN BURGESS PLAYS THE GREAT HIGHLAND BAGPIPE
Expressive pipe music by a premier piper.
05125* $7.95

SCOTLAND VARIOUS

ANDY STEWART, COME IN
All your favourite vocals, including Danny Boy and Amazing Grace.
06008* $8.95

KENNETH McKELLAR IN SCOTLAND
A collection of old and new Scottish songs with some originals by Kenneth McKellar.
06009* $8.95

TREASURES OF SCOTLAND
Peter Morrison, David Solley, Ron Gonnella, The Tartan Lads and others in a tribute to the National Trust of Scotland.
05113* $7.95

GREAT SONGS OF SCOTLAND
David Solley sings classics such as Skye Boat Song, Scotland the Brave and Harry Lauder Medley.
05076* $7.95

THE TANNAHILL WEAVERS
Folk tunes and bagpipes by a rollicking Scottish group.
03101 .... $9.95

PETER MORRISON MEMORIES
A selection of Scotland's favourite tunes by this great singer.
06005* $8.95

ALL THE BEST FROM SCOTLAND
Various artists include Stuart Anderson, Lomond Folk, and David Solley.
05100* $7.95

THE ROBERT BURNS SONGBOOK
A delightful selection of Burns songs by various artists.
05092* $7.95

PURELY PIOBAIREACHD
Solo classical Pipe Music by Seumas MacNeill.
05041* $7.95

POSITIVELY PIOBAIREACHD
Another classic solo album, this one by Donald MacLeod.
05089* $7.95

GRANT'S PIPING CHAMPIONSHIP
Award winning piobaireachd from this top competition. Cassette only.
06001* $8.95

* **CASSETTES** – ALBUMS MARKED BY * AVAILABLE AT THE SAME PRICE AS THE LISTED ALBUM.

CHAPTER THREE

Your First Rough

The Dummy

What are you going to sell? The very first step in drafting a catalog is making a product list. Again it is always best in my opinion to include all possibilities. You can always eliminate items later.

Your first product list might just contain the name and price of an item. I found it useful to arrange products by category. I would set up a few sheets of legal paper with a different title on each and then add potential products to the appropriate list. The categories I used were: Books, Records, Jewelry, Clothing, Highland Attire, Music, Gifts and Special Orders. I spent the first two or three sessions just brainstorming on possible items for the catalog. Much later on in the process, as I edited the list down to a final selection, I added the codes and a basic product descripton to each item, as well as the name of the supplier for that item.

Product selection for a catalog is a much trickier business than it is for a store. In a store you can order a few of an item and test the market. If they sell you order more. If you are out of certain items you can replace them with new things to show your customers. If you order a few items and they don't sell you can put them on sale and try something else.

In a catalog you must plan months ahead for items and you must anticipate their sales. You need a lot more cooperation from your suppliers. You need a lot of inventory on hand as well as assurances from your suppliers that they will hold some backups for you. If an item is a loser, you are often stuck with a lot of them and, as mentioned previously, Murphy's Law states that you will always run out of your big hits.

In the gift business it had been fairly common to mark catalog items up the same amount as store items. As a rule of thumb you doubled the cost of an item to get a retail price. If you paid $10 for an item, you sold it for $19.95 or $20. Because of the skyrocketing costs of catalogs, it is not unlikely that the same $10 item will now be listed for $24.95 or even $29.95! I have seen more than one company go through the entire process and expense of setting up and mailing a first catalog only to find they had priced themselves out of any chance of success. If you are overpriced relative to the market, you lose since most customers will buy elsewhere. If you are underpriced relative to the cost of the product you sell you lose since you are not going to make enough profit to pay the overhead.

You need to milk every bit of profit you can out of an item without going overboard. It is a tricky business that does not follow all the rules of normal store buying. Many small catalogs take pricing for granted. They establish a price and that's that until a significant change occurs in the product cost. You must constantly be aware of your competitors and you must constantly look for ways to make a few cents here and a few dollars there. When it's all said and done, the little savings and small extra profits are what will decide if you make money or lose it.

Your next task is to come up with a basic list of products that you might sell. As you start your first list you might find this collection of dos and don'ts helpful.

Product Selection

1) Choose products that show well or that have a benefit you can describe.
2) Try to be unique.
3) Choose products that give you a reasonable profit.

4) Make sure you can get resupplied with an item if it takes off and sells more than expected.

5) Consider how the manufacturer might help you if you put his products in your catalog. Many manufacturers will provide photos, copy, extra discounts or special bonuses, but you have to ask.

6) Exclusives sell very well and give you greater latitude in markup since no one else has the product. Many manufacturers will let you run a product for six months before it is released to other stores. Or you may be able to have a slight change made to an item, thereby making it exclusive. You should also look into having items made for you or making them yourself.

7) Consider how the product fits in with your image. Is it worthwhile to sell an item that may produce a few extra bucks, but cheapen your image? Sometimes you may enhance your image by offering a product even if you don't expect to sell many.

8) An old retail trick that still works, if used correctly, is the loss leader. Sometimes you can make no profit at all on an item, but the sale of that item "for a loss" enables you to sell other items that you do make money on (more on this later).

9) An industry rule of thumb is that in any catalog ⅓ of the products will be big sellers, ⅓ will be average and ⅓ will be losers.

10) If your product is unique, you don't need a large selection of sizes, colors, etc.

11) If your item is not unique, you should consider a large selection of sizes or colors or some other innovation.

12) Sale and discount items have a place in every catalog and you should plan for them, not just let them happen as an afterthought.

13) Some items may be too inexpensive to merit inclusion in your catalog. Think of combining these items with more of the same or like items. For example, instead of a jar of jam selling for $2.95, show a set of three jams for $8.95.

14) In the long run all items must justify their space. The more money an item makes for you the more space it can be allocated.

15) If you really feel strongly about an item, even though it seems to break all the rules, give it a shot! Some of my biggest successes violated all the rules but I had a feeling about them. Rules of thumb are only rules of thumb. I must also point out that some of my feelings that violated all the rules were also big mistakes! There are no guarantees.

16) Consider how you will ship each item. Some items can be so much trouble to ship that the labor involved eats into the profit. Ask me some day about the seven-foot pole ax!

17) Consider how you will store each item. Some items can demand more attention than they are worth.

18) You should only choose items you have samples of on hand. Never select items that are not yet manufactured. If an item is not manufactured on time, you will be in big trouble. I have suffered some of my largest losses because of nondelivery by suppliers. I've lost money and customer good will.

Now that you have a working list of the products you may sell in your catalog, you are ready to start your first rough. For this you need a few pencils, erasers, a ruler and a pile of inexpensive paper. This rough work is a time to experiment and be very loose. It's O.K. to be sloppy. At this stage you should be throwing a lot of paper away.

You want to start by pulling your list of products into groups, such as books, clothing, records, etc. Perhaps you can use a theme so that all nautical items are together, all hiking paraphernalia, all electronics. Some current catalogs mix item selection and organize by what looks good on the page. You can mix and match; there is no one correct way but you must remember that you are trying to hold your customers' interest. Consequently, you must have some idea about who your customer is.

Now I am going to let you look over my shoulder as I set up a rough dummy for one of my early catalogs. I have given you a general idea about what we sold and what I thought my customer profile was. Let me expand on that description and explain some of my product selection. It is nothing more than brainstorming.

I am going to stay away from fancy upscale Scottish and Irish clothing even though it sells very well in our shop. I don't think I can show its strong points without color and top quality photography to get across texture and luxury. I am also going to down play the Waterford crystal because it is done so completely and inexpensively in the Shannon catalog. I can't match their prices or selection and I think serious Waterford buyers would be familiar with that catalog.

I will do at least two pages of records and two pages of books. No one else is pushing them; they are easy to ship, easy to store and supplies seem pretty good. I will emphasize genealogical and heraldic connections in all products. I think people want to say, "This is my family tartan," or "that's the Hollan coat of arms on the door knocker."

I will push our range of hard-to-get items in Highland clothing since we stand almost alone in the field. These products are interesting and I think people will sense that we are authentic when they see them in our catalog.

I will push descriptions over art since I can't afford a lot of photography and I think our customers appreciate a lot of explanation and background.

I think that a man's kilt is the item that many hard core ethnic buyers will use to evaluate our prices. I don't think these buyers remember all the prices of all the other gear, but the kilt is usually the most expensive, so they focus on it. I think if they find the kilt expensive, they will assume all of our prices are expensive. If the kilt is reasonable they will think all of our prices are reasonable; consequently, I am going to sell my kilt for only a few dollars more than it costs and feature it somewhat as a loss leader. At present, the wholesale cost of a custom-made man's kilt is about $140, and the few places selling them charge between $250 and $395 retail. I will sell mine for about $150!

Why? Because a man buying a kilt needs to get all the other items that go with it if he wants to look correct. You don't wear sneakers and a sweatshirt with a tuxedo! He needs kilt hose (long socks), flashes (garters), sporran (big hairy purse worn in front), bonnet (several styles), skean dhu (knife tucked in kilt hose), kilt pin, kilt belt, brogues (laced shoes) and maybe a casual tweed kilt jacket or a fancy formal kilt jacket. He could add a few other items of jewelry, and if he wanted to be fancy, I even sell swords and sword belts.

All these items were properly priced so that I made my full profit. Generally a customer ordered his kilt then went ahead and ordered all the other stuff with it. It was common to sell a kilt for $150 (my profit $10), then sell $800 or more of stuff to go with it (my profit $400 to $500). Do you get what I mean by a loss leader now?

To make up for the lack of quality paper, graphics, photography and color in the catalog, I am going to be very folksy and chatty. I will include tid bits of information, recipes, informative articles and appear more like a newsletter than a catalog. I need to make small and interesting work for me.

You now have my basic philosophy, for want of a better term. I have summarized what I'm going to sell and how I'm going to sell it. I have a list of products and a pile of paper. It is time to start on the first rambling rough draft.

The First Rough

Most catalogs are paged in multiples of four because it is an easy and inexpensive way for machines to print pages called "quartos." So, begin by taking a piece of typing paper and folding it in half. You now have a tiny booklet of four pages. A quarto simply means four pages are printed on one sheet. If you use two sheets of paper, you have eight pages, etc. I arbitrarily decided my catalog would be 32 pages (that is eight quartos). This is a fairly standard size and I felt if it didn't work out I could change it. I've also decided to use an 8½″ × 11½″ page size which is a common size for catalogs. Dig through your pile and you will see what I mean. I want to use the most common size since just about every printer is set up to run it and you can get the best price.

EXAMPLE 6

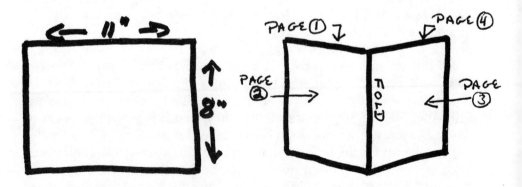

In my young stupid days I wanted to be a little different, a little better. When I computerized my business I decided to get a custom inventory and accounting program rather than an off-the-shelf system. Rather than spend $500 for the package system, I spent $800 for the custom. By the time I finished fiddling to get that custom system working correctly four years had passed and I must have paid over $5,000 to a programmer. It never did work as well as the $500 off-the-shelf system I eventually bought.

What's the point? Don't try to make your catalog a little larger or smaller than one of the two or three standard sizes. If you go outside standard formats, your options go down as your prices go up. STAY WITH STANDARD FORMATS. If you want to get cute and inventive, do it with copy or graphics. Look at different formats after you've run seven or eight catalogs.

For the first stage I take 32 pieces of blank paper and I write FRONT COVER on one of them and BACK COVER on another and put these two pages aside until later. Great! Now I only have 30 pages to go!

I number the other pages starting with the inside front cover which is page 2. For my first seven or so catalogs I could not afford to bind in an order form. I just made one of the pages an order form that the customer was supposed to cut out and mail in. I chose one of the two center pages for this purpose and made the back of this page available for general announcements or a sale item since it would disappear with the order form when sent in.

For this catalog sample we're working on, I decided to use two pages of books and two pages of records. For now I'll put them towards the back. I want at least one page for the kilt since I am making such a big deal out of it, and it does require a lot of explanation, i.e. how to measure and how to wear it.

On this first draft I don't draw items, rather I title pages and start filling in the goods from my list of products. I end up with an idea of what will go on what page. I start conceptualizing what goes with what and where it should be in the catalog. Below are a few examples of these rough outlines from an early catalog.

As you see these are just lists of what items may go together on a page. I start to see groups forming. I start to see the feature item on a page. I outline until I get a sense of what should be collected together,

JEWELRY COLLECTION
(IRISH)
CLADDAGH STORY -
RINGS   EARRING
PENDANT   STICK PIN
GOLD CLADDAGH
KIDS CLADDAGH

SHAMROCK STUFF
EARRINGS -   PINS -
NECKLACE -   BROOCH -

ST. BRIGID'S CROSS
ROSARY ???
                BIG TARA BROOCH
(24)

JEWELRY COLLECTION
(SCOTTISH)
CELTIC NECKLACE - BIG $45
SASH BROOCH $35
PENDANTS:
SINGLE + DOUBLE
ROYAL PENDANT ?? MAYBE
THISTLE STORY -
THISTLE EARRING
  "   NECKLACE } SET?
  "   KILT PIN } PRICE?
KILT PIN GROUP:
-CROSS
-SWORD
-AX
-RAM
(25)

GIFTS - Both Countries
COINS - ELIZABETHAN
-SCOTTISH
- IRISH
TEA STRAINER | FARM CLOCK
LAP ROBES | MUGS ??
  -TARTAN | -THISTLE
  -TWEED | -SHAM.
BUTTONS | WALKING STICKS
SHOE BUCKLES | IRISH BLACKTHORN
THIMBLES: |
-SHAMROCK | SCOTTISH
-THISTLE | CARDS
LION UMBRELLA | (NEED 2-3 PAGES!!)
(26)

EXAMPLE 7

then I start to doodle. I can't draw to save my life but these are rough sketches to give me a sense of space and proportion.

I have six heraldic items that I know should be shown together. They range in price from $25 to $95. I also know that I need a general explanation about the procedure for ordering a family coat of arms so that we can deliver the correct item. Example 8 shows two preliminary doodles for that page.

After working on my preliminary product list I came to realize I needed a page of bagpipe items. The page had to show a set of bagpipes ($295), a "teach yourself the bagpipe kit" ($40), four different practice chanters ($15 to $75), a book and an instructional cassette. Examples 9 and 10 show two sketches for potential layouts. Notice they are not very detailed, yet each gives a good idea about how things should be arranged. I like having a few choices at this stage so once I get a rough layout, I usually make a few variations. You keep any variation that looks half decent at this stage.

For many of the layouts I often copy a layout from one of the catalogs in my pile and start replacing the items they use with my items. Then I might change this a little and that a little until something seems to work. I don't try to finish a page at this stage; I just get good ideas about what works and what doesn't. I don't fill in copy. I just put lines where it will go. I'm trying to figure out how the art works at this stage. How I will show things. How the pages relate to each other. I

EXAMPLE 8

 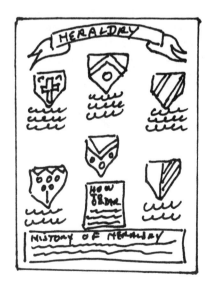

 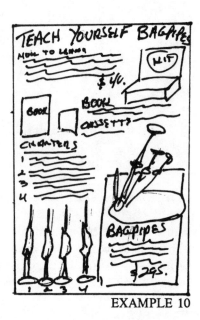

EXAMPLE 9   EXAMPLE 10

almost always work with two pages at a time. The two pages that face each other are seen as one element by the reader.

I continue doing page sketches until I have a rough layout of the whole catalog. I may have not included a few items or shown some things more than once at this stage. I usually don't have anything on the covers yet and the order form is still a blank, but I'm getting a rough idea about what's going to go where. Some of the pages may have two or three possible layouts and some pages may be 75% complete with a big empty box in the corner. That's all fine. This is a sketch. I am thinking with my pencil. Try to rough out some pages. Let them sit a bit and then go to some of your first detail work.

CHAPTER FOUR

The Front Cover

Let me boil down a few books' worth of cover philosophy into one sentence: Use the front cover of your catalog to capture your kind of customer. People today are getting a pile of catalogs in the mail along with bills, flyers, letters and other promotions. They often sort this pile next to a wastebasket and many won't even open a catalog if it doesn't grab them immediately. All the work and planning, all the expense of layout and printing, all the cost of shipping and postage, are losses if the potential customers don't even open your catalog. You've got about two seconds to get their attention and keep your catalog out of the wastebasket.

I believe the front cover should give a strong enough impression of what your catalog is about so that your type of customer will open it. I don't believe the cover is the place to sell products. I believe it sets the mood and immediately tells the customer what kind of business you are. Many experts argue for the other side of the coin. They say the cover is the most noticed part of the catalog and you should sell there. It seems many office supply and discount catalogs hold to this philosophy. As you flip through your catalog cover file you will have to make up your own mind. Should the cover sell products or a mood?

Now is the time to start thinking about your cover. Whom do you want to reach and how will you reach them? Do you want to look upscale or bargain basement? Do you want to look very professional or do you want to look folksy and down home?

Now is the time to start looking for cover art. For my first catalogs I saved a bundle by finding art in several places. You can use illustrations or photos from books you are selling. There are now volumes of clip art in libraries, bookstores and even stationery supply stores. Many manufacturers are delighted to supply you with free photos of their products, most of them are professionally shot. Sometimes an enlargement of a detail can be spectacular.

As you think about the look of your catalog you should also be thinking about your logo. The most distinctive feature on the cover will and should be your company name. Many professionals urge you to run your name in the same style and colors from catalog to catalog so the customer will come to identify it immediately.

Look at some of my early catalog covers. The first four covers shown are all black and white. The art for Example 11 was a sketch of my shop copied from a photo onto graph paper. I can't draw very well but this looked enough like my shop to use it. The title was from press type purchased for $3 at the stationery store. I let the printer talk me into printing the title out of register so it would be more interesting. I'm sorry I agreed since the final product looked blurred to me. Example 12 was a blow-up of an Irish postcard we were selling in the catalog. Notice how our company name looks better without the fancy treatment.

Example 13 is a copy of a print from the 18th century. Again a free piece of cover art since no copyright was involved. I used the same logo but dropped it to the bottom of the page. Finally, in Example 14 I featured many of the products for sale inside the catalog and changed the logo, adding a cutout of a piper.

In 1985 we used our first color cover (Example 15). Only the cover quarto was color. That means the front cover and page 2 as well as the back cover and page 31 were color. The rest of the catalog was still black and white. We used the inside covers to show clothing items we thought would benefit from color. The graphic was an illustration by N. C. Wyeth from one of the books we were featuring inside the catalog and the logo has changed once again. Example 16 is a blow-up of a detail from a book. It is a copy of the royal arms and was quite handsome in full color and a sky blue background.

For some reason I decided to change the logo again and came up

EXAMPLE 11

EXAMPLE 12

Scottish & Irish
Imports Ltd.

FALL/WINTER 1983
$1.00

EXAMPLE 13

SPRING/SUMMER 1984
$1.00

Print reproduced from the book
The Clans of the Scottish
Highlands by Robert Mclan.
See page 33.

Scottish **&** **I**rish
Imports Ltd.

EXAMPLE 14

Scottish & Irish Imports Ltd.

FALL/WINTER 1984

$1.00

EXAMPLE 15

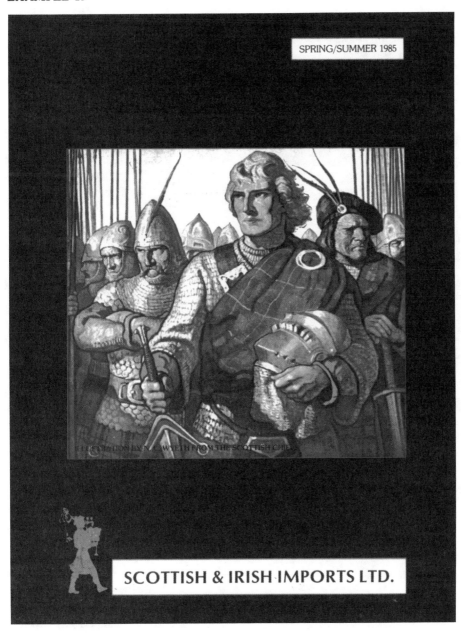

EXAMPLE 16

FALL/WINTER 1985

DIEU ET MON DROIT

SCOTTISH & IRISH IMPORTS LTD.

EXAMPLE 17

EXAMPLE 18

EXAMPLE 19

EXAMPLE 20

EXAMPLE 21

Fall 1988   Two Dollars

SCOTTISH & IRISH
IMPORTS · LTD.

EXAMPLE 22

with the mess found in Example 17. It looks to me like we are called Scottish & Irish Simports! I guess the reason I'm showing my dirty laundry in public is so you will be encouraged. You will probably look at some of these examples and say, "I could do better than that."

Each catalog was picking up more color pages inside as we found we could afford them. The catalog shown in Example 18 is our first full color catalog. We had professional help with this one and it shows. You can see that we have gone for a mood photo on the front and we have changed our logo again (for the last time).

Examples 19 through 22 are follow-up covers I've included here so that you can see how we continued developing. Hopefully they will convince you that everyone can get better with a little time and effort.

When you finish this chapter you should go to your front cover clip file and start reviewing the covers you've collected. Can some of the formats you see work for you? Can you use any of the frames or borders? Can you use a similar layout with some variations?

Do you have the skills to start playing with a logo for your catalog? If not, you may find a typesetter with some ideas. A graphic artist specializes in this sort of work but may be too expensive for you at first; whereas, typographers often have books full of samples that may be easily adjusted to your needs for very little cost. Even home computer programs for newsletters and art have headline formats that are quite attractive.

Keep playing with cover ideas and variations. This is the most important page in your catalog. It deserves extra attention.

To Sell Your Catalog Or Give It Away?

Some people charge for their catalogs. Some catalogs are almost works of art in themselves. There are not many of these but a few exist and the limited group of people willing to pay for them are usually quite satisfied.

Some catalogs are not very attractive but they are so specific that collectors are willing to pay for them. These catalogs often have no photos. In fact they are often just mimeographed pages. I myself subscribe to a few such catalogs dealing with my interest in military miniatures and antiquarian books. It would be rare for these catalogs to have more than a thousand paid subscribers on their lists.

The vast majority of catalogs are free. "But wait," you say. "I see a price on most catalogs, including yours!" That's true but the price is there for other reasons.

1) It gives the appearance of more value. People are getting something worth a dollar or two for free.
2) It enables book stores to sell your catalog.
3) It allows compilers to sell your catalog in magazines.
4) In some states there is no sales tax on products for resale.

If you are not a highly specialized catalog that caters to a small group of subscribers (e.g., antique toy soldiers), do not plan to sell your catalog. You want as many customers as possible and you will pay to get them, not vice versa.

CHAPTER FIVE

The Back Cover

The main purpose of the back cover is to get the catalog to your customer. It is the place you put your customer's name and address. It is also where your company name and address go. It is often the part of the catalog your customer sees first. It is one of the two most important pages in your catalog. As much as I believe you should not usually sell products directly on the front cover, I believe that you must sell products on the back. In fact, the back cover is often the best selling page of a catalog. Look at the back covers in your clip file.

The back cover should certainly portray your company image, but you should also be selling here. You can sell products directly by giving all the ordering information or indirectly by giving some information on the cover and referring the customer to the inside of the catalog for more information. It can also be used successfully for special promotions or sale items.

The back cover must fill a number of technical requirements. It must have the postal permit indicia. This is the little box with the words "Bulk Rate, U.S. Postage Paid" and a location, company name or permit number. The indicia works something like a stamp and lets the post office know who pays. We will discuss it in more detail in the chapter on mailing.

The back cover must have room for your customers name. In general it takes a label of some sort, either a peel-off label that is returned with the order form or a cheshire label, which is less expensive and is not

EXAMPLE 23

If you are interested in starting your own Scottish & Irish
Imports Store drop us a line, we can help.

Scottish & Irish Import, Ltd.
197 Main Street, Annapolis, Md. 21401
Attn: Mr. Jim Hollan

A. THISTLE WREATH PIN. The symbol of Scotland is exquisitely portrayed on this lovely wreath of thistles delicately dotted with Amethyst colour stones. 2" diameter.
#287022 - $29.95.

B. TARTAN TIE. Put plenty of pizzazz in your wardrobe with our 100% wool tie with a pure silk tip. Wears extremely well without wrinkling after repeated knottings. Available in stock. Select from every Tartan listed on page 17. Please specify Tartan number when ordering. Imported. **#621 - $11.95.**

C. TARTAN BOW TIE. Comes pre-tied in a perfect bow with slim adjustable neckband that fits comfortably under your collar without bulking. Available only in names listed on page 16. Imported. **#65 - $8.95.**
(Please specify Tartan and number when ordering.)

D. STAFFORDSHIRE ENAMEL BOXES. Recapturing all of the charm of the 18th century craft, Staffordshire Enamels are designed and produced in England with the same care and imagination that created their demand in the 18th century England and France. Enamel is fired to etched copper and decorations are hand painted. Each piece is presented in a gold blocked case together with a certificate of authenticity. *Thistle* **#182111,** *Shamrock,* **#182112 - $95.00** each.

E. BALMORAL. This traditional headgear with a red and white diced or plain band is usually worn with a clan crest badge, *(see page 20.)* Sizes 6-7/8 - 8. Imported. *Diced,* **#740436,** *Plain,* **#740446 - $45.00** each.

SCOTTISH & **I**RISH
I M P O R T S · L T D.
197 Main Street, Annapolis, Md. 21401

removed. If you look closely you will see many catalogs have a message just above or below the label that says something like "or current resident," "or current occupant." If this message is included your catalog will stay at the address to which it is mailed. In specialized catalogs the message may be more specific. For example, if you were mailing catalogs of textbooks to bookstores, you might append the message "or current book buyer."

Later in this book you will learn about mailing lists. You will learn about testing the results of lists. One way of doing that is to determine if the addresses are current. You probably have noticed that many other catalogs have a message that says "address correction requested." The labels on catalogs marked this way will be returned to you if they are no longer correct, enabling you to update your mailing list; however, you must pay the return postage. The flip side of the coin is that you will not send a new catalog with new mailing costs to the same address the next time.

Example 23 is a fairly basic back cover from one of our catalogs. You can see the required elements: the indicia, the space left for our customer label, and our company name and address. In this case I was cleaning my in-house mailing list so I used an address correction notice. I sold items directly from the back that I thought also set the mood for the kind of catalog we were. This was a very successful back cover for us. After many edits and proofreadings you assume you've caught all the mistakes. If you look at our address under the logo, you will see we spelled Annapolis wrong! I love mail order!

As you flip through your back cover clip file you will notice that a few basic layouts seem to occur with some regularity. Rather than try to come up with a whole new approach to back covers, I suggest you take one of these layouts and adapt it to your own use. You don't even need to decide which products you will use yet, you just want to get a rough layout developed for your catalog.

If you choose my Example 23 as a layout you want to copy, some variations might be similar to those shown below. Again I am trying to give you a sense of how the rough drafting process works and experimenting with ideas will prove very useful to you.

EXAMPLE 24

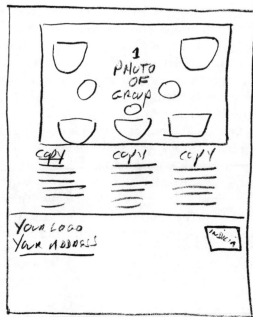

CHAPTER SIX

The Order Form

If you open up your order form clip file you will see that order forms fall into a few basic patterns and you will more than likely choose one of these patterns and copy it. You will notice that key elements repeat from one form to the next. You must make it as easy as possible for your customer to order. You must also make it easy for the customer to order the correct item. Careful planning at this stage will enable you to reduce the number of costly returns and exchanges.

I mentioned earlier that I could not afford to bind in an order form for my early catalogs. Since you may have the same limited funds I did, examine the order form in example 25. We used the entire page and made our boxes and lines for descriptions roomy enough for ease of writing. If the spaces are too small, it is a problem for the person making the order as well as for the person receiving the order. I created this order form myself with graph paper, ruler, black marker and some press type. It was a boring project but saved a lot of money.

On the back of the order form (Example 26) I put our guarantee and information about orders and damaged merchandise, as well as a blurb asking for customer referrals. I also used this space for a personal message or news item. In this case I included a photo of our pipe band and a few words about their going to Scotland to represent the U.S. at the World Championships. It made the page useful and personal.

When you look at Example 27 you see our bind-in order form. It is smaller yet clearer than our old form. The back (Example 28) features a

EXAMPLE 25

SCOTTISH & IRISH IMPORTS, LTD.
197 Main Street
Annapolis, Maryland 21401
PLEASE PRINT CAREFULLY, THIS IS YOUR MAILING LABEL

FALL/WINTER 1985

SHIP TO:
Name _____
Address _____
City _____
State _____ Zip _____
Daytime Phone _____

SOLD TO: (if different than ship to)
Name _____
Address _____
City _____
State _____ Zip _____
Daytime Phone _____

☐ Check or Money Order (Do Not Send Cash) • (Sorry, No C.O.D.'s) •

☐ Charge to My ☐ VISA ☐ MASTERCARD • SIGNATURE _____

Acct. No. ☐☐☐☐☐☐☐☐☐☐☐☐☐☐☐☐ • Exp. Date _____

Customer Number (from mailing label) _____

your customer number allows us to process your order more quickly

CREDIT CARD ORDERS • CALL TOLL-FREE • 1-800-638-0430
Monday-Friday 10:00 a.m. - 6:00 p.m. E.S.T.

Md. Residents Call 301-267-7094
Information and Inquiries Call 301-267-7094

HAVE YOUR ORDER, CHARGE CARD AND CATALOGUE READY

ITEM NUMBER	QTY.	OFFICE USE ONLY	DESCRIPTION	NAME OF TARTAN	COLOUR OR TARTAN NO.	SIZE	GIFT BOX $1	PRICE EACH	TOTAL PRICE

GIFT CARD MESSAGE:

SHIPPING, PACKING & INSURANCE
For Orders Totaling:
UP TO $25.00 - Add $3.00
$25.01 TO $50.00 - Add $3.50
$50.01 TO $75.00 - Add $4.00
OVER $75.00 - Add $5.00

PRICES ARE FOR CONTINENTAL U.S.
NO ORDERS WILL BE PROCESSED WITHOUT
SHIPPING, HANDLING & INSURANCE

TOTAL PRICE OF ITEMS
IF SHIPPED TO MARYLAND ADD 5% SALES TAX
SHIPPING, PACKING & INSURANCE

TOTAL AMOUNT ⇨

THANK YOU FOR YOUR ORDER

EXAMPLE 26

GUARANTEE

It's very simple. You must be completely satisfied or return the item within two weeks for exchange or full refund. Exceptions: we cannot refund or exchange soiled or worn merchandise, or articles custom made to your specifications.

POSTAGE

Sorry folks but we must receive the postage, packing and insurance charges to process your order. Our charges are identical to most national mail order houses and you can be assured with prices what they are today, we do not make a profit on these fees. Since we carefully wrap and insure all items, it costs almost the same for us to ship a $5 map as it costs to ship a $50 book. We urge you to avoid delays on your order by sending the correct amount.

GIFTS

Your gift orders will receive our special attention. If you would like your gift purchases sent directly from our store to the recipient, just enclose their name and address with your order. We will ship directly to them and include a card saying the gift came from you. If you wish us to send to more than one address, please add the additional postage.

BACK ORDERS

Except where "special order" is noted, we almost always have every item in stock. If there will be a delay, you will be notified: we only hold back orders with your permission.

CHARGE CARDS

Custom made and special order items will be charged to you at the time you place your order. Back orders will not be charged until shipping date.

PRICES

We argue and kick and scream with our suppliers, shippers and customs agents when it comes to cost; consequently, we believe we offer you the very best quality for the price. We plan to hold all prices in this catalogue through January 1, 1986, if possible.

DAMAGED MERCHANDISE

Yes, it is insured! If you should receive broken or damaged merchandise, SAVE THE BOX AND CALL YOUR LOCAL UNITED PARCEL SERVICE OFFICE. They will arrange to pick up and return the merchandise.

Page 20

THE SCOTTISH & IRISH IMPORTS PIPE BAND.

PLEASE SEND A CATALOGUE. If you have friends or club members who would like to receive our catalogue, just send us their addresses or your membership list.

As we go to press, our Championship Scottish & Irish Imports Pipe Band is travelling to the World Championships in Scotland, where we will represent the United States. We want to congratulate all the members of the band on their remarkably successful season, and wish them the best on their European tour.

Name _____

Address _____

City _____

State _____ Zip _____

Name _____

Address _____

City _____

State _____ Zip _____

Name _____

Address _____

City _____

State _____ Zip _____

BAND DISCOUNTS

We do offer discounts on volume orders for Bands, Clubs and Fraternal Organizations. We are particularly helpful when it comes to organizing Pipe Bands. Drop us a line outlining your needs or problems.

**ORDER TOLL-FREE
CALL
1-800-638-0430**

© Copyright 1985 Scottish & Irish Imports Ltd.

Don't Save This Page!

Many of you don't like to use the order form since it leaves a page out of your catalogue. Well don't worry, every time you order, you receive a new order form with your shipment. To help us process your order, please use our order form to order if possible. Credit card orders, call toll free 1-800-638-0430. If you call please have your Visa or Master Card and your catalogue handy. For information, please call 301-267-7094.

Scottish & Irish Imports Ltd.
197 Main Street
Annapolis, Md. 21401

sale item and includes the guarantee and other necessary ordering information. Most importantly a return envelope is attached. Does this increase returns? You bet it does; that's why we pay more money to do it this way.

Example 29 shows how the order form is made from one piece of paper and folded by the printer. Since an order form is a job almost anyone can do, I urge you to try laying it out yourself based on examples in your clip file. I recently talked to a colleague who had an agency design and paste-up an order form for his new catalog. With the exception of using his logo, address and phone numbers, the form looked pretty much like most others to me. The cost for this design and paste-up job was $2,400! I think he could have done it himself for $50, or if he had designed it in pencil and had a typesetter set it and paste it up, it may have cost $100 to $150.

As a final note, you should know that there are printers who specialize in order forms. I was intimidated by my lack of printing knowledge when I did my early catalogs, and in my ignorance I believed it would be easier and cheaper to have one printer do everything. That is not especially true. Printers often specialize in a few things and may use other printers for certain tasks. Printers are not bothered about shipping vast quantities of paper all over the place. We will go into more detail about this under the chapter about printers but you should be aware that you may be using more than one printer for your catalog. I found I could have my order form printed in another state, shipped to my catalog printer and bound into my catalog and still save a substantial amount of money. Why? Because the people who made the order forms had very expensive machines that specialized in that type of operation.

As you work on your order form plan, I would like to repeat an earlier piece of advice: Keep it easy to use.

EXAMPLE 27

SCOTTISH & IRISH IMPORTS, LTD.
197 Main Street
Annapolis, Maryland 21401

Use peel-off label from back cover whether or not address is correct. If incorrect or if you're moving, fill in below. If you receive duplicate catalogs, please attach all extra labels.

PLEASE PRINT — GIVE STREET ADDRESS — WE SHIP UPS

SHIP TO:
NAME
ADDRESS
CITY
STATE _____ ZIP
DAYTIME PHONE

CREDIT CARD ORDERS
CALL TOLL-FREE
1-800-638-0430
Monday-Friday 10:00 a.m.-6:00 p.m. E.S.T.
Md. Residents Call 301-267-7094.
Information and Inquiries Call 301-267-7094
HAVE YOUR ORDER, CHARGE CARD
AND CATALOGUE READY

SOLD TO: (if different than ship to)
NAME
ADDRESS
CITY
STATE _____ ZIP
DAYTIME PHONE

ITEM NUMBER	QTY.	OFFICE USE ONLY	DESCRIPTION	NAME OF TARTAN	COLOUR OR TARTAN NO.	SIZE	GIFT BOX $1	PRICE EACH	TOTAL PRICE

GIFT CARD MESSAGE:

SHIPPING, PACKING & INSURANCE
For orders Totaling:
Up To $25.00 —   Add $3.00
$25.01 To $50.00 — Add $3.50
$50.01 To $75.00 — Add $4.00
Over $75.00 —   Add $5.00

PRICES ARE FOR CONTINENTAL U.S.
NO ORDERS WILL BE PROCESSED WITHOUT
SHIPPING, HANDLING & INSURANCE

TOTAL PRICE OF ITEMS	
IF SHIPPED TO MARYLAND ADD 5% SALES TAX	
SHIPPING, PACKING & INSURANCE	
TOTAL AMOUNT	

METHOD OF PAYMENT   Check or Money Order (Do Not Send Cash). (Sorry, No C.O.D.'s)
VISA / mastercard   Charge to My ____ VISA ____ MASTERCARD Exp. Date ____
Acct. No.
SIGNATURE

THANK YOU FOR YOUR ORDER

NAME
ADDRESS
CITY
STATE _____ ZIP _____

PLACE
STAMP
HERE

SCOTTISH & IRISH IMPORTS, LTD.
197 Main Street
Annapolis, Maryland 21401

EXAMPLE 28

GUARANTEE

It's very simple. You must be completely satisfied or return the item within two weeks for exchange or full refund. Exceptions: We cannot refund or exchange soiled or worn merchandise, or articles custom made to your specifications.

POSTAGE

Postage charges include shipping, packing, and insurance fees. These fees are the same as those of other national mail order firms and are the exact price we pay. Since we carefully wrap and insure all items, it costs almost the same to ship a $5 map as it does to ship a $50 book. Please be sure to include the correct amount with your order, so that there will be no delays.

GIFTS

Your gift orders will receive our special attention. If you would like your gift purchases sent directly from our store to the recipient, just enclose their name and address with your order. We will ship directly to them and include a card saying the gift came from you. If you wish us to send to more than one address, please add the additional postage.

BACK ORDERS

Except where "special order" is noted, we almost always have every item in stock. If there will be a delay, you will be notified: we only hold back orders with your permission.

CHARGE CARDS

Custom made and special order items will be charged to you at the time you place your order. Back orders will not be changed until shipping date.

PRICES

We have made every effort to hold down the costs of supplies, shipping, and customs duties in order to bring you the very best quality for the price. We plan to hold all prices in this catalogue through June 30, 1989, if possible.

DAMAGED MERCHANDISE

Yes, it is insured! If you should receive broken or damaged merchandise, SAVE THE BOX AND CALL YOUR LOCAL UNITED PARCEL SERVICE OFFICE. They will arrange to pick up and return the merchandise.

BAND DISCOUNTS

We offer discounts on volume orders for Bands, Clubs and Fraternal Organizations. We are particularly helpful when it comes to organizing Pipe Bands. Drop us a line outlining your needs or problems.

COMMANDO SWEATERS
These tough, wool ribbed sweaters are not only comfortable but extremely durable. Matching fabric patches trim shoulders and elbows. Carefree yet sensible in all natural 100% wool, in navy and khaki. Imported from England. Sizes: Men – 40, 42, 44 & 46. #524 - **$65.00.**

CLOSE OUT SALE $49.95

PLEASE SEND A CATALOGUE.
If you have friends or club members who would like to receive our catalogue, just send us their addresses or your membership list.

NAME _____

ADDRESS _____

CITY _____

STATE _____ ZIP _____

NAME _____

ADDRESS _____

CITY _____

STATE _____ ZIP _____

EXAMPLE 29

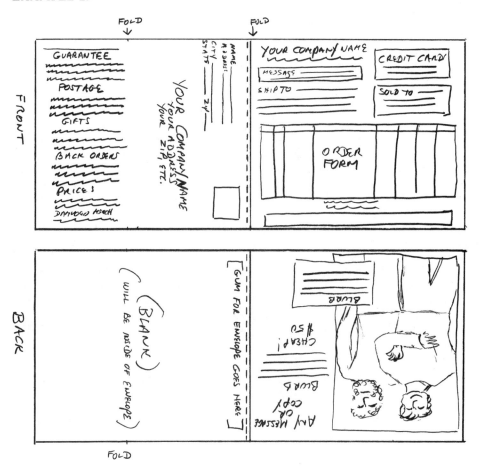

CHAPTER SEVEN

Art and Photography

Should You Hire a Professional or Do It Yourself?

Before you decide to do your own photography or hire it done, you should investigate the availability of free art. Ask every supplier you have for art or photos of their products. Many suppliers pay a lot of money to have their products photographed by professionals and they are pleased to loan photographs. After all, the more you sell, the more your supplier makes.

I have asked suppliers for photos and more than once had them say, "You know, so and so also asked; maybe we should have some made up." A few weeks later I've received photos to use. If they don't have photos they may have line art, drawings, old ads or something else they have used for promotion. Ask! You may be amazed at what you get.

In addition to your suppliers, you can get wonderful help from government agencies, travel agencies and archives. We needed some background photos of castles in Scotland as well as general country views. We got all we needed for free from the British Tourist Board. Local archives, libraries and historical societies are usually a rich source of mood and background material for free.

Clip art and border books are available at most book or art supply shops. These are handy for dressing up forms, page layouts, creating borders, and making dull pages interesting.

SHOULD YOU HIRE A PROFESSIONAL?

A professional photographer will charge in the range of $500 to $1,000 a page. A cover photo will often run more. Having said that, I am familiar with catalogs that have spent over $5,000 a page for photography. If you decide to use a professional, you may be able to find a price a few hundred dollars less per page, but let me give you some guidelines.

1) Make sure your photographer has commercial and product experience. Anybody can shoot a pretty sunset or a cute kitten. It takes a lot of skill to shoot crystal goblets or a silver tea service because of reflection problems.

2) Have they done catalogs? I would be worried if they haven't. If they are going to learn a new skill by shooting your catalog then you should be getting a huge price break. Why? Because your catalog will go into their portfolio and they will be able to charge the next client more as they now have catalog experience.

3) Get references and check them. Ask the references if the photographer met all deadlines. Ask what they liked and about any problems they had. Ask if they would hire the photographer again. I once had someone say, "No, because I'm using a new photographer." I got the name of the new photographer and ultimately hired him.

4) Have a clear understanding of deadlines and make sure you both meet them. You must be punctual if you expect the photographer to be punctual.

5) I recommend that the first time you contract for a portion of your catalog for a photo shoot. For example, you may have the photographer shoot four pages of jewelry. If that goes well you may shoot the next section of four or six pages and so on until you are comfortable.

6) The photographer should have a studio. If not, it should be clear who will pay for studio or equipment rental.

7) Have a clear understanding about who owns negatives and when they can be used. Get this in writing. You will save a lot of money by using photography from catalog to catalog.

8) If you find a good photographer, count your blessings and keep the friendship going.

9) Don't confuse amateur with professional. A friend or relative who ". . . is into photography," can be a curse. The world is full of these well meaning amateurs and they can cost you a bundle. A person may know how to shoot a wedding or a night scene under low light. Very few professionals even deal with commercial and catalog photography. Be careful.

YOU ARE THE ART DIRECTOR

Unless you have hired one at additional cost you are the art director. That means you decide what the photo will look like, what background will be used, what props will be used, which way an item will be shown. If you plan to use a live model, you must decide what will be shown and what clothing is appropriate. What color shoes, which type of blouse, what jewelry should be worn. You do not go to the photographer with a pile of goods and say, "Make these look nice." The art director plans each shot completely. You want the products arranged and shown properly. You need an ironing board and pins to make clothing look just right before shooting. You need to plan ahead of time for the best use of props, models and time so that you don't have models standing around doing nothing while you're paying them.

Before going to the photographer, you should have a sketch of each photo you want the photographer to take. It should be clear enough so that the photographer knows how to position each photo even when you are not there. A successful photo shoot is based first on successful planning.

When you plan your photos make sure that you consider how the backgrounds blend. Consider not only the layout on the page you are working on but the page it will be facing since an open catalog is seen two pages at a time. Teach yourself to be an art director as you examine your pile of catalogs.

SHOULD YOU DO YOUR OWN PHOTOGRAPHY?

Even if you have never taken a photo, you should at least think about being your own photographer. Cameras are so user friendly and affordable these days that it is an option to be considered.

Since you are not shooting a high fashion New York catalog, you could get by with a good quality 35 mm camera, a good quality 50 mm lens and a close-up lens. Based on your needs a telephoto might also be useful. A tripod, three lights with stands, a backdrop paper holder and a few rolls of backdrop paper (black, white and gray) will complete the basic camera and studio setup. Total cost—under $500—if you are frugal and shop around.

I do much of my own photography, but don't use my own darkroom anymore as these services are so readily available and it frees my time up for shooting. During a photo session, you shoot the entire roll of film and ask the photo store to print a proof sheet for you. This is an 8″ × 10″ sheet of paper with all the photos from a roll on it. With a magnifying glass you pick the best photo and have it enlarged, usually to 5″ × 7″. You can tell any decent photo store how to crop or manipulate your photos for you; moreover, much of the cropping can be done when you send your pages off to the printer.

The basic studio set-up I use lets me cover most shooting situations. It usually takes me about 15 minutes to set the lights and backdrops up and I store everything in a closet when not in use. Even if you decide to have more difficult photos shot by a professional you can still shoot many simple photos yourself. I've listed some basic set ups and tricks I've learned with my camera:

1) Books and records should be shot straight on then crop the final photo to the edges of the book or record. This means the background doesn't matter since you will trim it all out. You will often get glare and reflections from lights. My technique is to lay the book or record on the floor near a window. I don't let the sun shine directly on the item. With standard black and white TRI-X film I usually have plenty of light to shoot the book or record and rarely have any reflection. I stand on a step ladder and shoot straight down.

2) Keep the backgrounds simple; in black and white photos the back-

ground can often be very distracting. I use white paper and an old white sheet often. Most things look good against white. Conversely, I also use black paper and some black cloth for those things that don't show well against white.

3) A very simple but effective backdrop for small items is a piece of cloth on a desk or table; drape the cloth over a box or some books for height. Shoot in natural light or place spotlights to each side so they throw light at an angle. After looking through your camera, adjust the lights slightly until you get the effect you want. See Example 30.

4) You can shoot a lot of things with a paper holder and a roll of backdrop paper (purchase at photo stores). You can set up for small gift shots as well as full body shots of models. Example 31 is a sketch of the basic set up I use.

5) Start shooting photos early in your schedule and put the photos you may be able to use aside. Don't forget to shoot photos of items that are backups for the catalog. You may need them one day before going to press when you have to knock out an item for some obscure reason. You will thank your lucky stars if you have prepared for such an emergency.

EXAMPLE 30

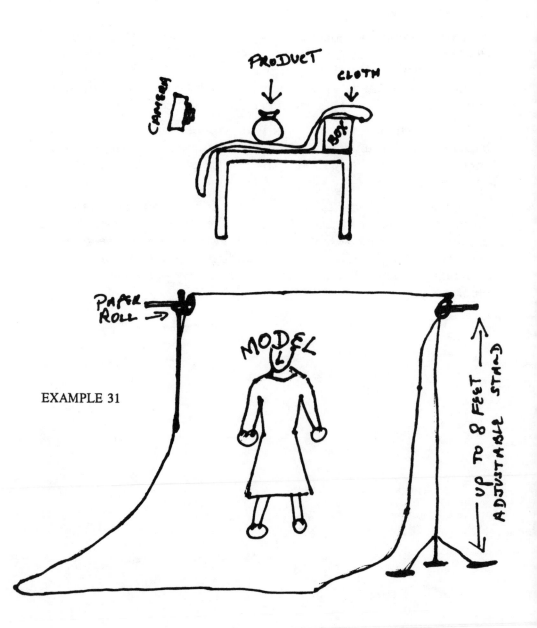

EXAMPLE 31

CHAPTER EIGHT

Copy

A Lot More Than Words

You should know your audience better than anyone else; therefore, you should know best how to communicate with them. Some people like lots of description and technical data while others need very little description. It is up to you to decide just what your customers need to know in order to buy your product.

Copy should point out the benefits of a product. If your price is better than anyone else, push savings as a benefit. If your price is about the same but you have a better selection, you should push choice as a benefit. People need to know why they should buy something. Will your product make them smarter or thinner or popular with their peers? Copy is not just description, it is your saleman. Let's take a new book and write some samples of copy for it:

COPY A—The Home Improvement Manual—A new book about improvements for your home and basic repairs with illustrations. 325 pages, 285 illustrations $24.95

COPY B—The Home Improvement Manual—Just Released! This remarkable book is crammed with clear and easy-to-follow illustrations that enable anyone to make hundreds of home repairs and improvements. You can save thousands of dollars by doing it yourself with this easy-to-use manual. Order fast! 325 pages, 285 helpful illustrations $24.95

Clearly the facts are the same, but copy B sells while copy A only describes. Copy B shows a number of benefits and creates a sense of urgency by suggesting the customer "order fast." Why? Are you going to sell out? Who knows? The sense of urgency is created by telling the customer to do something now. It took me about two minutes to write copy B as a quick example of selling. I don't have any doubts that B would sell a lot more books than A.

It is best to begin by writing all you want to say without worrying about space. Go back later and edit. Then polish the edited version. It is always easier to edit things out than it is to add things in.

People don't read catalog copy the same way they read a book. When you write copy you can repeat things from box to box. Customers are not going to read each and every piece of copy, therefore you do not need to slave over making every description different. That is not to say you list every item as "fantastic" or a "great savings," however, it is O.K. to repeat yourself more than you would normally. Look for some of these patterns in your pile of catalogs.

I relied very heavily on copy to sell our products. I made a point of establishing a friendly tone, almost like a letter home to the relatives. We said why we liked a product and even said why we didn't like a product! We would find an older copy of a record that completed a set and would report that the quality wasn't very good but we featured it for the hard core collector. Our customers really appreciated that information and tended to trust us more.

I also used copy to educate our customers. We found many customers were unsure about what was worn with what for a complete Highland outfit; consequently, we featured a whole page explanation of all the clothing items. I can't tell you how many people wrote thanking us for the information. We received numerous requests from clubs, newsletters, newspapers and even a few small magazines asking for permission to reprint that page. (Every one of those reprints was free advertising for us!)

Copy has its own flow and rhythm. Before sitting down to write copy, I find it helpful to spend fifteen minutes reading a lot of other copy straight through, not pausing to analyze it. This usually gets all the adjectives and adverbs flowing and prepares me to dig into my own copy.

As a final note, remember that copy needs to inform and it should sell, but never lie or intentionally mislead your customer. Not only is that wrong but it's also bad business. People aren't stupid!

Example 32 is the advertisement that so many people thanked us for or asked permission to reprint in their newsletters. It is also a good example of how one black and white photo can be used effectively with copy flowing around it.

EXAMPLE 32

The Highland Collection
Scottish & Irish Imports Ltd.

Gentleman's Guide to Correct Scottish Attire

Who wears what when? When you buy traditional Scottish attire from our Highland Collection we want you to wear your outfit year after year with complete self-assurance. We offer you this guide so that you will always be correctly attired.

All mens Highland attire is classified as one of two types — "Daywear" or "Eveningwear." These two classifications have nothing to do with the time of day you wear them. "Daywear" is a synonym for casual wear. If you would wear slacks and sport shirt or a suit then "Daywear" is correct attire. When a Tuxedo is called for, then "Eveningwear" is correct.

KILT The most recognized and basic item in a highland wardrobe, the kilt should be no longer than the bottom of the knee and no shorter than 2 inches above the kneecap. The sides and back of the kilt are pleated and the front, or "apron," is left plain.

SPORRAN There are no pockets in a kilt so a purse or "sporran" is attached by a belt to the front of the kilt. They are made of leather for "Daywear" or fur for "Eveningwear." Full head sporrans of muskrat, badger, or raccoon are correct for day or evening wear. The long white horsehair sporrans should only be worn by pipers or officers in Highland Regiments.

HOSE Since the kilt comes to the knee, long socks called "Hose" are needed. Daywear Hose can be white or any solid colour. Whereas eveningwear should be white or Tartan to match your kilt.

FLASHES These are garters that wrap around your calf to hold up your hose. They come in solid colours to coordinate with your kilt. These are not called "Flashers" — which are old men in raincoats often found around bus stations.

SKEAN DHU Means "black knife" and is worn tucked into the top of your hose. It is an anachronistic item that is still a must if you are to be correctly dressed. Horn is for daywear and jeweled tops for eveningwear.

GHILLIE BROGUES Any general shoes are fine for daywear and black dress shoes or pumps for eveningwear; however, Ghillie Brogues are the traditional footwear for day or evening.

PRINCE CHARLIE COATEE This is a formal jacket worn for eveningwear. Tweed jackets are worn for daywear.

BELTED HALF PLAID This is not really required for eveningwear but it is often added for a dramatic sweep of Tartan. It is fastened under the jacket and pinned to the shoulder. Full plaids are worn by pipe bands and regiments.

BONNET The two main styles are the Balmoral (shown in photo) and the Glengarry. Both styles come plain or with a checkered band called "dicing". A Tartan band is not traditional on a bonnet. The choice of bonnet is one of taste not correctness. A bonnet should never be worn without a clan badge which is pinned to the cockade.

PLAID BROOCH This fastener for the belted plaid is usually of ornate design for an elegant finishing touch.

Labels on photograph: Bonnet · Cap Badge · Plaid Brooch · Belted Half Plaid · Prince Charlie Coatee · Sporran · Kilt Pin · Kilt · Skean Dhu · Flashes · Hose · Ghillie Brogues

PAGE 3

CHAPTER NINE

Your Second Rough

The Hollan Bag System

With the work you did on the first draft, you should now have a rough outline of your catalog, the number of pages, what products are likely to be on those pages, and a sense of what you might do with the covers and order form. Now it's time to start refining your rough sketches. As you refine you can and should change things. It is the rare bird that jots everything down the first time and then changes nothing.

You must now start collecting bits and pieces of copy, art, pricing and code information, as well as roughs and sketches. Before you go any further it is necessary to have a system of organization. Having tried various and sundry systems and methods at great personal expense, I've settled on the "bag system with the box variation."

If you have a 32-page catalog in mind, get 32 paper bags, preferably white, although kraft paper is fine. You want bags that allow you to write on the outside and they must be big enough to hold an 8½" × 11" page without folding. I generally use a bag about 11" × 15". These are readily available at most gift stores at a minimal cost. If you have a separate order form, make sure you have a bag for it.

Now number each bag in the upper right hand corner. Page 1 has the subhead "cover." As you gather information, art, copy, roughs, comments or anything else to do with a page, file it in the proper bag. I also keep a list on the outside of the bag as work progresses so I know the bag contains its rough draft, then later its final draft, codes and pricing checked, copy complete, typography complete, art complete, all complete. Late in the process when most bags are done I flag problem bags with red marks that say "Need new photo," "Missing copy," etc.

This is an extraordinarily simple procedure and it works like a charm. You won't believe what a mess it is to have 32 pages of catalog material spread out in an office and not arranged by pages. Talk about a nightmare!

After you have bagged your work, I suggest you go to a stationery supply store where they sell cardboard file boxes. I use one made by Acorn that is approximately 12" wide by 10" tall by 15" long. I think I paid about $4 for it. It holds all the bags, my pencils, pencil sharpener, rulers, blank paper and my clip files. This is my portable self-contained mail order office. When I want to work at home I just take the whole box; I'm never missing anything. I've been in the offices of very expensive and very uptown graphics people and watched then run all around trying to find items they had "just a minute ago." You can't beat the old box and bag system!

Now that the secret of my elaborate filing system is out let's start developing the rough drafts into a second draft stage. To start, you should work on two pages at a time, not one. Why? Because you are inclined to focus on the one page you are working on but an open catalog really shows two pages at the same time; consequently, you must keep a page in balance with the facing page.

The cover is always considered page one and is not numbered, therefore even number pages are always on the left and odd numbers on the right when facing each other. If you get wild on page 8 and use a large black background with fancy white reversed type, the effect might be diminished if page 9 is fairly ordinary. Thinking of page 8 and 9 as a unit will enable you to enhance special effects and graphics.

As you arrange products on a page you should be aware of a concept called square inch analysis. In a nutshell, the idea is that the space an item takes on a page should correspond to the dollar value of sales that item generates. For example, if you have two items on a page and one takes up 40% of the page and the other takes up 60% of the page, as a

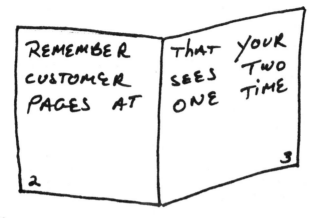

EXAMPLE 33

rule of thumb the one taking up 40% of the space should generate 40% of the sales and the one taking up 60% of the space should generate 60% of the sales. Although you do not know what an item will sell relative to others on a page when you put a new catalog together, you should at least attempt an estimate. This type of analysis will prove invaluable as you put your second and each successive catalog together.

The same principle holds from page to page. One client I worked with had two pages of posters shown in his catalog. Each page displayed six posters that sold for approximately $9 a piece. He was very proud of the look of these pages. Another page had a few items jammed together, shown poorly and overcrowded. An analysis of the pages from his own figures showed that the crammed page was generating a profit of almost $22,000, whereas the poster pages were losing approximately $1,900 since the cost of the two-page display was more expensive than the income generated by poster sales.

The client loved the look of these posters because they were pretty and he felt he needed a large space to show them properly. He also pointed out that he sold a lot of these posters. What he failed to do was find out how many posters he needed to sell per page in order to justify the display space. Since a poster only netted $5 gross profit he needed to sell thousands to make a profit.

Conversely, the crammed page had some items he felt sold themselves, therefore they didn't need a lot of display. He had crowded together a few excellent sellers in the belief that they needed no special presentation. I eventually convinced him to cut the poster display down from two pages to a third of one page and spread the cramped material on two pages. This left him with two-thirds of a page he could use for new items. Most importantly, the improved display of the good sellers increased their sales. This single alteration changed his three-page profit from approximately $20,000 ($22,000 minus $1,900) to $78,000! This illustrates how important it is to have a sense of the cost and income of each page and product. It also illustrates how important it is to constantly fine tune your catalog. We will consider square inch analysis in detail later in this book when we discuss evaluating the success of your catalog.

Once again I think the best way to learn how a draft takes shape is to look over my shoulder as I do a few pages. Let's start with some sporrans. These are the pouch-like purses worn by men to the front of the kilt. It is a very specialized item and usually hard to find. We have a good selection and we keep them in stock. We want to push this fact since it distinguishes us from our competitors. A kilt without a sporran is like a tuxedo without a tie.

The first thing I did was decide that I was going to sell sporrans in the catalog and I added the names of the 17 different sporrans we stock to my preliminary product list. At stage one I just named each sporran and jotted its price down on a piece of paper under the list title "Highland Attire."

After my product lists were developed, I kicked around a lot of ideas about sporrans and how to display them. I had no models to follow from my sample catalog pile since it's a product one hardly ever sees. What I did do was look at similar products and see how they were shown in various catalogs. In this case I focused on purses and pocket-books. I noticed from the way others showed them that the major angle for photos was straight on and props were not really necessary to show the item well.

I took my pencil and a few pieces of paper and started doodling with different arrangements. Some typical doodles are shown in Example 34. **A** was the first obvious answer and really not a bad solution to the problem. It accounts for 16 of the 17 items which means I could use the extra for an emergency backup and since they are of similar size the grid works proportionally. In step **B** I'm taking the idea in **A** a step further. I added outlines of the sporrans and lines for copy below each. I have just started and I already have a working solution but I will keep doodling. **C** is a variation of **B** but I have knocked out two boxes in order to put in a headline and some description about sporrans since many of my customers don't know what they are. This would make it necessary to drop two more sporrans from the display, but make the page more interesting in my opinion.

My first draft stage ended with the quick sketch of **A**, **B** and **C**. When I came back for the second draft I had a great starting point for this page. I could have gone ahead and used the layout in **C** and just started choosing which sporrans would go where and start writing copy. I liked the layout in **C** but I was worried because many of my first draft pages had little boxes in grids (remember my early record and book layouts in Chapter 2) and the catalog was getting a very boring feeling.

The second draft started with this rough evaluation of the first draft. If it was boring I would try to develop it a bit more so I tried some graphic variations. **D** was another variation of **C** with an attempt to eliminate the grid from the page. **E** was an attempt to arrange the photos into two group shots. **F** was another variation using one photo of all the sporrans in the center with copy around it.

I liked **E** and **F** best and started playing with them. As I started to develop them I had a hard time figuring out how to shoot the group shot without making everything cluttered. A professional would have been able to do this with a large format camera but I was trying to save money and take the photos myself. I also was wondering if I had to include as large a selection as I was showing.

I decided to go for the layout in **D** and feature 11 sporrans. I could shoot these photos easily myself and the layout was clear and easy to follow without being another grid. I then drew a more detailed sketch of the page to size so that I would get a better feel for it.

This sketch (Example 36) went into my bag labeled page 10. I knew that I was going to use 11 sporrans so I went to my list and chose 12 out of the 17 available, 11 that I would need and one spare in case I had a problem at the last minute. Then I started drafting copy. The copy

EXAMPLE 34

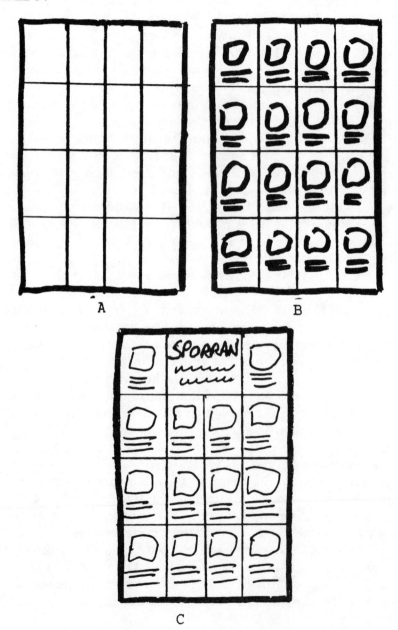

A

B

C

EXAMPLE 35

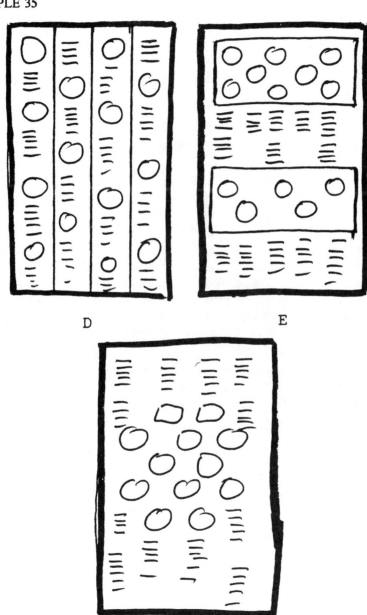

D   E

F

included the code number, the price and a brief description of each sporran.

I wrote out my copy on a legal pad, making sure to label the page in case it got separated. When I finished, the page went into the bag with the page sketch. Example 37 is a hand written copy page so you can see what it looks like and how I just mark my corrections on it as I edit and re-edit.

The bag for page 10 now contains a detailed outline of the page as well as the unedited copy, codes and prices. I have a very good idea about the photos required to complete this page. I consider this a very good second draft.

The layout of a page may be determined by any number of factors. Remember I told you to ask your supplier for photos of products you want to show. I received some spectacular photos from one of my clothing suppliers and an additional discount for featuring his products in my catalog.

Now I had to approach the layout differently. I had to make the photos fit the page. The photos were of three different clothing items, with one model in each photo. We were already selling these three items in our shop and we knew that they all did well, but one of the three sold as much as the other two combined. I already had a rough layout for the facing page which was fairly square with photos on the inside of the page and copy running down the outside. It seemed to me that the logical layout for the new page would place the photos on the inside with copy on the outside. This resulted in the following sketches in Example 37.

I settled on layout **C** which gave the most space to the best seller. I was undecided as to what item I would feature in the bottom corner as I knew I did not need all the space available for copy. As it happened I later settled on a light motif throughout the catalog of photos of Scotland and Ireland. The space saved for an unknown product turned out to be ideal for one of these.

The photos of the merchandise came from a supplier and the photo of the castle came from the British Tourist Board. All the art for this page was free. Not bad. Example 39 shows the finished page.

You should now turn your rough sketches into more finished products. You should start using your ruler to measure up pages and get a

EXAMPLE 36

EXAMPLE 37

PAGE 10 - SPORRANS

(A) PRINCE CHARLIE SPORRAN — THIS RICH BLACK PONYSKIN AND RED LEATHER BACKING (WITH RED LEATHER BACKING? COMBINE TO MAKE A STUNNING EVENING WEAR SPORRAN. THE SILVERPLATE THISTLE design ON THE FLAP IS BACKED BY genuine RED LEATHER. SIX TASSLES hang FROM THE FRONT. THE FLAP OPENS TO A ROOMY POUCH. IT COMES WITH A MATCHING BLACK LEATHER AND CHROME CHAIN BELT.
CODE 77201. . . . . $ 125.00

(B) THISTLE SPORRAN — THIS THREE TASSLE BLACK LEATHER SPORRAN FEATURES A SILVERPLATE THISTLE design CANTLE OVER GREEN LEATHER. THE TASSLES ARE CHASED AND finished with A REPOUSSE (spelling?) THISTLE. The pouch has A BACK FLAP FOR STORAGE
CODE 77101. . . . . $ 125.00

(C) ROB ROY — THIS UNUSUAL ALL LEATHER SPORRAN IS A COPY OF A VERY EARLY SPORRAN STYLE. THE RICH BROWN LEATHER IS ESPECIALLY SOFT AND PLIANT. POUCH STYLE WITH A DRAWSTRING FRONT. BELT INCLUDED.
CODE 77206. . . . . $ 65.00

better ideas where things go. This is the time to make sure your codes and prices are correct and to draft a lot of copy. It is not time for a finished product or final decisions to be made.

If something isn't working don't throw the page out. I find it better to start again and again if necessary but save your mistakes in your bag. I've sometimes ended up with five or six variations of the same page that still wasn't working. When this happens, I take a break, come back and lay out all the pages. Sometimes the collection of wrong approaches looked at together show me the correct approach.

You are still drafting and editing. Nothing is set in concrete yet. You have many clear cut tasks that need to be performed and each completion or refinement is leading you to a finished product. The second draft stage should include all the changes until the final draft and paste-up.

I urge you to prepare a few more items than you will need for your catalog. You will almost always run into last minute problems and it is certainly helpful to have a standby in the wings. If you don't need the extras you can use them in your next catalog.

After your first catalog, you will develop certain habits. I started to make a point of putting samples of potential catalog items aside as soon as I came across them. Whenever I found time I would poke through this growing pile and try some copy or a photo. When it came time to start the new catalog in earnest, I often had a number of items already blocked out.

Before we go on to the final draft and paste-up, let's look at some more technical aspects of the catalog and plan for our printing.

EXAMPLE 38

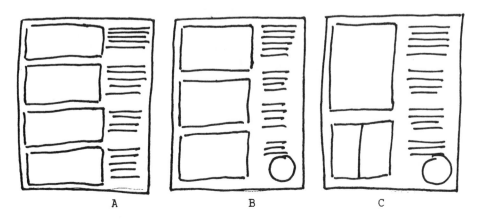

A B C

EXAMPLE 39

C. DUNNYDEER CIRCULAR PIN.
Duncan Hood has again captured the Scottish
landscape of sky and rocky cliffs in this very
unusual interpretation. Fired and glazed ceramic.
Each is a handmade original and may vary
slightly. **#20301 - $9.95.**

D. SCOTTISH THISTLES. Six Sterling Silver
Thistles are joined together to form a 1-½" brooch
highlighted by six sparkling Amethysts. **#284031
- $125.00.**

E.&F. CELTIC BROOCHES. The classic style of
Celtic knotwork is represented
in these two striking copies of antique brooches.
E. *Center Stone.* **#287029 - $29.95.** F. *Four
Stones,* **#287107 - $45.00.**

G. TAPESTRY IRELAND SCARF CAPE. Yards
of soft, luxurious, lightweight Irish wool are
handwoven in our combination scarf cape (the
scarf becomes a hood when you need it).
Stunning colors including Purple, **#56975,**
Dublin Blue, **#56972** and Aran White, **#56974 -
$195.00** each.

H. AUDREY. Wrap yourself up in yards of
luxurious soft woven wool. Our traditional cape is
styled in a loose, comfortable-over-everything, bat
winged style, topped with a long fringed scarf.
Color: Heather. One size fits all. Made in Ireland.
#569141 - $175.00.

I. TAPESTRY IRELAND SWEATER JACKET.
Once again a classic fabric is transformed into a
very special look in this stylish jacket. Made in
Ireland. Fully lined. **#569101 - $175.00.**

J. HELENA JACKET. These bold colors and
designs are an exciting departure from the more
conventional Irish Tapestry featuring dolman
sleeves, contrasting ribbed trim on collar and
cuffs and two slash pockets. Made in Ireland.
One size fits all. **#569151 - $175.00.**

TO ORDER CALL TOLL FREE
1-800-638-0430

9.

CHAPTER TEN

Printers

Your Best Friend or Worst Nightmare

Printers come in all sizes and shapes and they certainly have their share of saints and sinners. The best advice I can give you about printers is to ask lots of questions and compare them. I don't know what it is about people, especially men, that keeps us from admitting that we don't understand an explanation. It is imperative that you ask questions and understand the answers. Sometimes printers talk in their own jargon and if you don't understand an answer you should say so. If a printer treats you like an idiot, then dump him and move on. He more than likely is trying to cover up his own shortcomings.

A printer can do most anything you want—for a price. This section will give you some advice on choosing a printer and it will help you learn how to work with a printer so that you both benefit.

To start you must have the answers to some basic questions the printer will ask at your first meeting. If you can answer all his questions he can give you a firm bid on your catalog. This sounds logical, but it's not always that easy. The more planning you do the better, but first catalog makers usually have a lot of questions they want to discuss with the printer before making final decisions.

First, the printer will need to know the size of the catalog and the number of pages. Then he will want to know the number of photos since there is a screening charge for these. He will also want to know if you have any special items such as silhouettes (photos trimmed on the irregular outlines of images) or reverses (white areas black and black areas white). You should be able to answer these questions from your rough layouts and you should have the answers ready before you ever see a printer.

The printer will then ask how many catalogs you plan to print. We will discuss the size of the print run soon.

The next question the printer asks makes all the difference in the world in your costs. He will ask what kind of paper you want to use and you will stare at him blankly. There are people who only buy and sell paper for printing. It is a full time job requiring special knowledge and expertise. The ability to choose the right paper for a job at a good price can save you a bundle. I think trying to learn about paper at this stage is silly but knowing that your savings come here is important. What to do?

Show your printer a few sample catalogs that seem inexpensively produced but are of a quality you find acceptable. He will have a rough idea about what they are just by feeling them. Tell him that you are thinking about doing a catalog and you don't have a lot of money to spend. Ask for his suggestions. He will more than likely show you a few options. As he does, you will start to see that you are focusing on the qualities and weights of paper. Pay attention to the names of these choices: newsprint, 4 lb., 50 lb., etc.

You may want to do this with more than one printer face to face so that you can compare opinions. If a printer does not do your kind of printing he may recommend someone who does. After getting some basic printing information from at least three sources you should have a rough idea about the quality and type of paper you want to use and you are ready for your bid packets.

The Bid Packet

I don't care how small your catalog is; if you don't get a few bids on the printing job you are a fool! If you just want to throw money away, please send it to me. I can always use it.

You might think that printing bids will all come in fairly close together. Wrong! Wrong! Wrong! The range of quotes can be amazing. Printer A may have a lot of work and doesn't need a small job. Printer B may need the work but is not sure of the paper cost so he builds in a little margin for error. Printer C needs the work and has a warehouse full of paper that he needs to move. Some printers have a machine that lets them do your job cheaply and others do not. The variations are as endless as the quotes.

It is common with larger print runs to use a printer hundreds or thousands of miles away. In fact, a number of overseas printers advertise that it is cheaper to fly to Spain with your work, have it printed there while you spend two weeks on the Spanish Riviera, than to have it printed here.

I don't suggest that you travel overseas or all around the country for your first catalog, but I do suggest you look a little further afield than your own neighborhood. Go to the library and get the yellow pages for one or two cities near you and read the ads for printers. Many will say that they do catalogs. Copy addresses. You should find a minimum of six or seven sources. When we were in full swing we sent bid packets out to at least 25 printers on every job.

A bid packet is a clear description of what you want from a printer and a request that he tell you what he will charge for the work. Let's look at a bid packet for one of our early catalogs (Example 40).

As you can see the basic bid packet is a well organized outline of your printing needs for a specific job. If you have several different print jobs you would send a bid packet for each one. Before we go any further, let me explain a few things:

BINDING—Means the way the pages are held in the book. Many printers have their own bindery but some send binding out. You must get the bid for binding or you will have to add it to your cost later. There are three types of binding; Perfect—the pages are folded and glued in (most larger books); Saddle Stitch—a staple is driven through the center and holds all pages (this is the only choice for catalogs); Side Stitch— stapled through the side.

PACKING—Refers to the way the catalogs are delivered after printing. We are going to ship most of the catalogs to a nearby mailing house so they can go on skids, which are very cheap. We do however want catalogs for our shop and for some festivals we plan to attend in the next

Scottish & Irish Imports LTD.
197 Main Street
Annapolis, Maryland 21401
April 12, 1983

Bid Request for catalog—SCOTTISH & IRISH IMPORTS—FALL 1983
PAGE SIZE - 8 1/2" x 11"
NUMBER OF PAGES - 32
NUMBER OF CATALOGS - 40,000 please bid 50,000 also
PAPER - newsprint or similar quality
              40 pound coated stock inexpensive if available
ART - 109 photographs, 4 silhouettes, 2 pages reversed
BINDING - saddle stitch
PACKING - skids except for 6,000 in cartons
PICK UP/DELIVERY - will pick up cartons, remainder to mail house
DELIVERY DATE - september 5, 1983
ALL BIDS WILL CLOSE MAY 20, 1983

Yours,

James F. Hollan

EXAMPLE 40

few months. Since we have to move these and store them in offices we
want them packed in cartons (usually about 250 catalogs per carton) so
they are portable. This is a more expensive way to receive them but it
saves us agony in moving and storing so we happily pay the extra.
PICK UP/ DELIVERY—Refers to the manner in which catalogs will be
moved from the printer. In this case we plan to pick up 6,000 copies
ourselves; these will be in cartons and we will load them into our van
from the printers' loading dock. The remainder will be sent to our
mailing house by truck. We have not decided yet which trucking company we will use, but we can wait for that.
DELIVERY DATE—This is the date the catalogs must be ready to be
picked up. This is not especially the day they will be printed.

You can now send your bid packets out to printers. Give them
plenty of time to respond. Notice that we mailed our packet on April 12

and had a May 20 closing date. When you get your answers you will be surprised at the variety of responses. Price will not be your only deciding factor. As you eliminate printers down to a few choices, you can call them with questions. Let them know they are in the final selection group and you are trying to make up your mind. Ask them for samples of any similar catalogs they may have produced.

When you get down to your last choice or two, I have a trick I learned from an old retailer. He would take the best bid and call and say, "Listen, I like your company and I like dealing with you. Now all the bids have narrowed down to either you or Company X. I want to deal with you, but Company X is beating your bid by $500. Can you match that so we can do business?"

I must say in all the times I've used that trick, I never had anyone not match the number mentioned. It was never a lot of money but enough to give a small breathing space or make up for one of my mistakes.

If you are using a bind-in order form, you should get separate bids from each of the printers. You would also get bids from printers specializing in order forms. If you think you might use Printer X to print your order form and you want him to mail it to Printer A for binding with the rest of your catalog, make sure you ask Printer X to include the cost of shipping in his bid.

I cannot overemphasize the importance of shopping around and comparing printers. I am constantly amazed at the number of clients or colleagues who use a local printer because they are pals and the printer does all their printing (This usually amounts to some envelopes, business cards and maybe a flyer or two). They are too busy to shop around or too lazy. I know some of these local printers do nothing more than add in their markup and send the entire job off to a bigger printer in another town. I have seen clients pay more than double the fair cost of jobs for shoddy work and the privilege of dealing with another middle man because they were lazy.

Printers are people. I've had printers I would like to recommend for a Nobel Prize. Many have taken the time and energy to explain techniques, show me how to save money and keep me from slashing my wrists when I've screwed up. Some printers were not appropriate for my needs early on when we had small print runs, nevertheless, they took the time to help me along and put me on the correct path. In later years when we grew into a big account, these were the people I searched out.

Some printers are plain crooks, not a lot but enough to merit caution. The biggest problem is the group of printers that are just incompetent. In particular these are little guys trying to become larger guys and overstepping their abilities. The good news is you can avoid these types by getting lots of bids for comparison, looking at lots of samples of work and getting references for jobs similar to yours. As a footnote, let me state the obvious: A reference is no good if you don't check it!

Always have an agreement in writing with the printer you finally select. The agreement should contain a final version of the information covered in the bid packet and it should have a firm print date as well as a firm price. The earlier you book a job the better. In some cases it is mandatory that you book months ahead for the busy season. August is one of the very busy times for catalog printers and you will not be able to get press time with the best firms if you haven't booked months ahead.

You are probably getting the idea that catalogs require a lot of planning and long lead times. That is true; however, proper planning will save you a lot of money and it will minimize your mistakes.

CHAPTER ELEVEN

Mail Lists and Mailing

When your catalog is complete you will want to mail it to someone. Hopefully you have been collecting the names of people interested in your product and making your own mailing list. We collected names at Scottish highland games, Irish folk festivals. multi-ethnic festivals, etc. We would put out a list asking people to write down their names and addresses if they would like to receive our catalog. We started collecting names two years before our first catalog was even mailed! We got almost 7,000 names that way. We also wrote to Scottish and Irish fraternal organizations telling them what we were doing and asked for membership lists. Many responded and contributed another 1,500 names.

List Brokers

After you exhaust the obvious sources of names, you will need to turn to a list broker. List brokers deal exclusively in names and addresses. You tell them your needs and they find the right kind of names for you. They have names organized in more ways than you can imagine. They have names by sex, age, zip code and religious preference. They can get you subscriber lists, or donation lists, or lists of people who spent over $500 on jewelry by mail within the last six months. They can get you dentists or gym teachers. Their job is to find the right kind of names for you and they are very good at it. A list manager tries to market one specific list, but list brokers use everyone's lists. They make their money on commission from the list owners, not from you, the list renter. They want to make you happy, so you will keep coming back in the future. Use them well! Trying mail order without list brokers is like trying to climb Mt. Everest naked.

When you rent a list, you rent the right to mail your catalog to the names on that list one time and one time only. If you think you can just copy the names on a copier and use them again and again, don't even try it. All lists are seeded with decoy names by the list owner as well as the list broker. It is easy to catch a cheat and it is easy to take them to court. It is illegal to use names without paying for them.

When you rent a list, anyone responding to your mailing from that list, however, becomes your customer and that name can go on your growing list. Very general lists cost very little and very specific ones cost much more. Normally, you get what you pay for. You can rent a general list for as little as five cents a name; it may be only broken down by zip code and sex. Many people think this is handy for mailing to certain neighborhoods. I have never had much luck with this kind of list. They are often compiled from phone books and they give very little information about the potential catalog recipient.

The kind of person most likely to buy something through the mail is someone who has previously bought through the mail. The more recently someone has purchased an item through the mail the more likely that person is to purchase again. These two laws of the mail order trade mean names of buyers are the most expensive to purchase and names of recent buyers cost more than others. Each of these quantifiers is called a select and you generally pay a bit more for each select you choose. Careful consideration of your selects will cost you a few pennies more, but can save you a fortune in wasted mailings.

Better lists start at eight cents a name. These lists provide some information about the customer. Some specifics might be: subscribers to *Architectural Digest*, Book of the Month Club members, buyers from Fredericks of Hollywood.

Obviously, the very source of these names makes each list more valuable. Let's say you want to mail 10,000 copies of a new catalog of exotic nightgowns. Assume the catalog costs $1 each to produce and mail. You can rent 10,000 general names for five cents each for $500, or you can rent 10,000 names from Fredericks of Hollywood (for those of you that don't know, they sell lots of nightgowns). The Fredericks' names cost eight cents each for a total of $800. For your entire catalog mailing you pay $300 more for specialized names. Is it worth it? Do you think the added expense reduces the number of catalogs sent to people who don't care about nightgowns? Do you think the added expense increases the potential for sales by delivering catalogs to the correct type of customer? I sure hope you answered "yes" to both of those questions.

I just picked up this week's copy of a trade magazine called *Direct*. Here are a few of the lists advertised.

1) 88,049 subscribers to *Lose Weight Naturally*, a newsletter for people trying to lose weight.
2) 317,022 buyers of *Homeowners How to Book*.
3) 65,000 computer professionals (32 subsets)
4) 108,926 fourth quarter buyers of fashion wigs; mature women, average age 60; average sale $48.
5) 165,000 cycling enthusiasts who inquired about bicycle tours.
6) 95,000 visitors (mostly male) to the Basketball Hall of Fame and purchasers of NBA souvenirs from its gift shop.
7) 1,000,000 + names of Bloomingdale's by mail, selections include age, income, marital status, presence of children, types of goods purchased, etc.

That is just a brief selection of ads in one issue of one trade magazine! Are you starting to get the idea that there are lots of leads out there if you know where to look? The job of list brokers is to help you locate those lists. The brokers make their money from the commissions on lists used so you don't pay the broker for searching, only for what you use.

How do you find a list broker? Contact the Direct Marketing Association, 11 West 42nd Street, New York, New York, and ask for a list. You can check the ads in any of the trade magazines listed in the back of this book or try the yellow pages of cities like New York City and Los Angeles. I've also included the names of a few larger brokers in the Sources section at the back of this book.

When you get names from a broker, you will need to use a code so that you can identify the source of the name. When you test a list of names, you want to know what the response is. Some lists will work well for you and some won't. You need a system to evaluate these lists.

Let's say that we ordered three different lists from our broker and decided to test 5,000 names from each list. Let us use the code 1001 for List A, 1002 for list B and 1003 for List C. When people send in their orders, we will see the code above the names, or if they call, we will ask for the code with the order. (Yes, that's why they always ask for the code above your name when you place an order by phone.) As each order comes in, we will track it by code number.

Not only do we want to know how many orders come in from a certain list but we would like to know the average sale from each list. Why? Because List A might have a 3% return and List B only a 2% return. Does it sound like list A is better than B? You really don't know yet. It could be that the average sale for List A might be $20 whereas the average for List B might be over $150. A quick calculation on 10,000 names means list A would produce 300 orders (3% of 10,000) and List B would only produce 200 orders (2% of 10,000). Total sales of List A would be 300 orders × $20 (the average sale) or $6,000. The total sales for List B would be 200 orders × $150 (the average sale) or $30,000. You need to know rate of return *and* average sale to have a meaningful statistic.

A simple chart for this type of daily record keeping might look like this:

DATE	LIST A		LIST B		LIST C		TOTAL	
	Orders	Sales	Orders	Sales	Orders	Sales	Orders	Sales
Sept. 1	6	$286	6	$201	9	$410	21	$897
Sept. 2	7	382	4	131	11	417	22	930
Sept. 3	6	313	5	105	10	396	21	814

If you keep track of your sales each day you will quickly have a rough estimate on which lists are working and which aren't. As your business grows you might be tracking eight or twelve lists that you have used before while trying out six or seven new ones. Consequently, a good, basic, easy-to-read tracking system is very important.

Let's say that three months have gone by and sales activity has died down substantially. Look at the totals of the lists and evaluate them. Remember that we rented 5,000 names from each list and let's say they cost $500 each to rent. Your totals might look like this:

	Orders	Income	Average Sale
List A	168	$ 8,597	$51.17
List B	126	3,044	24.16
List C	211	9,081	43.04
Total	505	$20,722	$41.03

For many years it was common to discuss the percentage of return in conjunction with the average sale to evaluate the effectiveness of lists. If we continued that tradition we would say List A had a return of 3.3% (168 orders divided by 5,000 catalogs sent) and an average sale of $51.15; List B had a 2.5% return with an average sale of $24.16; and List C had a 4.2% return with an average sale of $43.04. We would base our decisions about which lists to reorder on those numbers and we would project sales based on those averages. Many catalogers still use this system but it is cumbersome since you must think in terms of return plus average and constantly juggle the two figures in your head.

Most people today look at these figures a little differently. They take the number of catalogs mailed (in this case 5,000 for each list) and divide that number into the total sales for each list. This gives them the income per book based on each list, as follows:

List A: $8,597 divided by 5,000 = $ 1.72 INCOME PER BOOK
List B: $3,044 divided by 5,000 = $ .61 INCOME PER BOOK
List C: $9,081 divided by 5,000 = $ 1.82 INCOME PER BOOK
TOTAL: $20,722 divided by 15,000 = $ 1.38 INCOME PER BOOK

You can use these figures to judge the effectiveness of each list against the others, and each list against the total. Just because a list is not as good as the others does not mean that it is not a moneymaker; conversely, the best list in a pile of losers is still a loser. Once you know what a list produces in its income per book you are half way to knowing if the list is profitable for you.

We will now add up all the costs of our catalog and divide by the numbers of catalogs mailed to get a cost per book. If it costs us $12,000 to produce and mail our catalogs than the cost per book is $12,000 divided by 15,000 catalogs or $.80 each.

So if our cost per book is $.80 each and our average income per book is $1.38 then we are making money. Correct? Sorry, no! We still have to take out the cost of the goods we sold. We will go through that procedure in detail later in this book but for now let's just say that our gross profit on sales is 60%. If according to our figures we sold $20,722 worth of goods, our gross profit is $12,433. Our total expenses were $12,000, so profit is $433. You would have made more money putting the $12,000 in the bank for six months!

Actually I set this example up to show you how a minor adjustment can substantially change your profit or loss. Go back to example 43 and determine what happens if everything else remains the same but you mailed all 15,000 catalogs to List A.

Expenses are all the same but gross income is now 15,000 catalogs × $1.72 or $25,800 and gross profit (60%) is now $15,480 before you deduct expenses of $12,000. Instead of a profit of $433, you now have a profit of $3,480.

If instead of List A, you mailed all 15,000 catalogs to List B with an average income of $.61 you would have gross sales of $9,150 and gross profit of $5,490. When you deduct the $12,000 of expenses you are now left with a loss of $6,510!

Do you see how one little test enables you to see your way into making money or losing money on your next mailing? It is critical that you constantly be searching for good lists, and you do that by testing. Often you will find a good list for your needs but one which is of a limited size. Should you use the same names over and over again? Yes, as long as they are generating a good return and good average sale. We used some lists 12 times or more.

I can't emphasize enough how important it is to keep careful track of your customer names with some sort of basic in-house code. These names will not only be of value as buyers from your catalog but you will eventually start letting a list broker represent your list and these names will generate money on their own. How much? It is not uncommon for names to generate $1 or $2 per name in rental fees annually. That means that if you have a list of 50,000 names, you could pick up

$50– $100,000 in extra income less approximately 20% in broker fees. Not bad for a bunch of names that are sitting around anyway! I've heard that some top lists produce over $7 per name and some of those lists involve hundreds of thousands of names. Companies are generating millions of dollars from list rentals alone. List management is another one of the new hidden industries that most people are not aware of.

Computers are now so inexpensive and user friendly that it is very easy to set up a small in-house mailing system. One pitfall to avoid from the beginning is failing to code your own names. The code does not have to be complex, but starting from Day 1 will save you lots of time later when you want your list to be most useful to the widest audience of potential renters. Some people only want to rent segments of your list, maybe only the women. If you can't break down your names by sex then that potential user of your list must go somewhere else. Your code will identify certain basic elements so you can sort the names at a later date.

Basic Mail Code

Here is a basic way to set up your house code for customers. Every order coming in to your business will get a code made up of nine spaces: You must fill in each space. Space Number 1 would identify the sex of the customers 1 = female, 2 = male, 3 = unknown. So, every code will have a 1, 2 or 3 in the first space. You determine the sex from the name or identifier such as Miss or Mr.

Make spaces 2, 3, 4 and 5 the date of the order. Spaces 2 and 3 will be the month with 01 = January and 12 = December. Spaces 4 and 5 will be the year—91, 92, etc.

Spaces 6 and 7 will record the frequency of purchases so that each time this customer orders the number will increase by 1. Spaces 6 and 7 will start at 01 for the first order, 02 for the next, etc.

Space 8 will be for the type of goods the buyer purchased according to a system you set up. For example, you may label food buyers as 1, clothing buyers as 2, book buyers as 3 and so on for any areas you want to identify.

Let's look at a few examples. If you get a first time order from a Mr.

James Hollan on March 24, 1991, for a cashmere sweater, his code should be 20391012

2 = male (Mr.), 0391 = March 1991, 01 = first order, 2 = clothing

If a Ms. Moore ordered some gourmet beer nuts on Nov. 12, 1991, then her code would be 11191011

1 = female (Ms.), 1191 = Nov. 1991, 01 = first order, 1 = food buyer

Now this is a very basic design. Obviously you can make a code to record multiple purchases, amounts of purchase, or anything else you can gather from the order. I used four product codes instead of one. That way I could record someone who bought a book, a record, some ties and a cake. Why bother? When someone wanted to rent all my food buyers I had them coded. The same person could also be rented to someone wanting all my book buyers or clothing buyers. Get it? It is not very complex, just a bit confusing at first.

Mailing Houses

When it came to actually mailing the catalogs, we were able to handle about 5,000 ourselves before going insane. When it comes time to mail your catalog, don't try to do it yourself. Professional houses can take your catalog, apply the labels, sort them by zip code and mail them a lot cheaper and more efficiently than you can. In general your catalog will go from the printer to the mailing house. Today many printers have their own in-house mailing facilities and you should ask your printer what he charges if he offers this service.

Before you actually order your labels, you must know who is mailing for you so that you can be certain the type of labels you get will go on the company machines. Labels can be ordered a number of ways, cheshire being the most common. They can come 4 up (meaning 4 across), 6 up, etc. The next most common type of label is a peel-off which usually costs about a penny more. This allows the customer to peel the label off the catalog they receive and stick it on the order form.

The benefit is that all the information, including the code numbers that you want for tracking, is already on the label.

A mail house charges a fee for bagging, zip sorting, and applying labels but it is hard to beat the prices. A rough rule of thumb for mailing a catalog would be about three cents per piece for all of these services. You would also pay for the postage up front at this point.

You should get a bulk mail permit from your local post office. These cost about $50 for a year and it will save you a bundle. It allows you to mail catalogs at a bulk rate as long as you mail at least 200 pieces and sort them by zip code.

As a final note, you must choose a mail house before you send your catalog to the printer. Then you can use the indicia of the mail house for the catalogs that will be mailed. The 6,000 catalogs we decided to pick up ourselves and give out at festivals or mail on our own later will not get an indicia. We just tell the printer to leave the indicia off these. You will see how in the section on paste-up.

It is important to start the process of choosing mail lists and mail houses long before the printing process begins.

CHAPTER TWELVE

Your Final Draft

You have reached that stage where you must make final decisions. You should have a bag full of information for each of your pages by now. You want to review everything and decide if you have things the way you want them. You can still edit and move things around but you must end up with a final layout for each page.

Once again I believe I can be most helpful to you by allowing you to watch over my shoulder as I edit final drafts from earlier catalogs.

I will dig into my bag for page 10 which is Example 35 in this book. I have written all the copy and I have double checked all the codes and prices. I'm still not crazy about the layout, so I decide on a few last changes.

I have not used any sort of headline and I would like to include a general statement about which sporran is worn when. I find I can do this easily if I drop one more sporran from the page and slide all the copy down just a little bit. But the page still seems a bit dull so I left everything where it was but boxed in a few items and used smaller headlines. The final product is shown as Example 44. This is from a very early catalog, and I use this page as an example since it was a great seller. It is not great design.

I recommend that you review the entire drafting process for this specific page. What was the goal? I wanted to create a page that would sell a lot of product. I also wanted it to look good but I had a very limited budget. Is it a great page? No. Is it a lousy page? No. Did it do

EXAMPLE 44

Sporrans For Day And Evening

FROM SCOTLAND

PRINCE CHARLIE SPORRAN
Rich black ponyskin and red leather combine to make this eveningwear sporran a real stunner! Silverplate thistle design on the flap is backed by red leather and 6 soft brown tassels hang down the front. Front flap opens to a roomy pouch. Matching black leather and chrome chain belt is included.
77201 Prince Charlie Sporran **$125.00**

THISTLE SPORRAN
Black ponyskin sporran features a thistle design silverplate cantle on a layer of red leather. The ferrules capping the soft brown tassels are detailed repousse' thistles. Pouch has back flap. Matching belt included.
77101 Thistle Sporran **$125.00**

EVENINGWEAR

RACCOON SPORRAN
A real showpiece! Large full raccoon head with pouch is trimmed with five brass tipped tassels tied with gilt braid for eveningwear. Belt is matching brown leather with brass chain.
7800 Raccoon with Tassels (evening only) **$275.00**
7801 Raccoon without Tassels (day or evening) **$195.00**

WHITE RABBIT SPORRAN
Coney fur, or rabbit, is a popular choice for eveningwear and a fine alternative to the more traditional, but illegal, sealskin. Our white rabbit sporran has black tassels, chrome cantles, thistle trim and a back pouch. Matching belt is black leather and chrome.
76002 White Rabbit **$45.00**

BLACK RABBIT SPORRAN
Beautiful black rabbit fur is trimmed with white tassels, chrome cantles and thistles. It has a back pouch and matching black leather and chrome chain belt.
76004 Black Rabbit ... **$45.00**

Sporrans are the pouches worn on the front of the kilt. There was a time when a Highlander would keep his ration of food here for a long trip, but today the sporran is used as a "purse" for holding keys, money, wallets, etc. As a general rule, leather sporrans are for daywear and fur sporrans for eveningwear, but there are exceptions. All of our sporrans come with a **FREE** matching sporran belt.

FOR DAY OR EVENING

SPECIAL

You can wear this handsome sporran with your daywear outfit, change jackets, and wear it again for evening. Double duty black leather sporran features a silverplate cantle etched with a Celtic design of interwoven birds and flowers. The leather is hand tooled with Celtic knotwork accented by chrome studs. We include the matching black leather and chrome chain belt.
77305 Celtic Sporran ...... WAS $95.00
WHILE THEY LAST **$79.95**

BLACK DAY SPORRAN
Many of you wrote and told us you needed a black daywear sporran to match your black kilt belts. This excellent choice is black pig grain leather trimmed with three chrome chains and balls with leather tassels, and comes with a matching black leather and chrome chain belt.
7605 Black Day Sporran **$40.00**

BROWN DAY SPORRAN
Three braided leather tassels highlight this popular day sporran. It's made of sturdy brown pig grain leather with a snap open front, and comes with a matching all leather sporran strap.
7301 Brown Day Sporran **$40.00**

DAYWEAR FAVOURITES

THE TARGE
This day sporran is handsome black pig grain leather intricately tooled with a Celtic knotwork design and accented with chrome studs. It opens to a roomy all leather pouch. We include the matching black leather and chrome chain belt
7504 Targe Sporran **$90.00**

THE ROB ROY
This unusual sporran is made of soft, supple leather gathered in a pouch style with a drawstring closing for lots of extra room. This is one of the earliest sporran styles. Our rich brown leather Rob Roy comes with a matching all leather sporran strap.
7302 Rob Roy Sporran **$65.00**

the job? Yes. Did later catalogs have a better display? Yes, but this worked and it was something to build on.

Helpful Guidelines for the Final Draft

1) You should make changes, doodle with ideas and try things up to the final draft.
2) You don't have to draft an entire page before you switch to another.
3) It is good to take a break between drafts of a page. It helps to come back later with a new focus.
4) If a question occurs to you while working on a page, don't be sure that you will remember to check it later. So many things go on in the creative process that I am always thinking of then forgetting things. If a question occurs to you, just jot it down on the page you are working on or on the bag for that page.
5) You don't have to be an artist to figure out what the art should look like or where it should go.
6) Never get too artsy. Remember you want to sell the product not the model or the background or the blurred soft focus effect that is lovely but hides the product detail.
7) You will make mistakes. You can be so intimidated by the fear of making mistakes that you will do nothing or you can accept the fact that mistakes will happen and you will learn from them. Go for it! He who hits more home runs than anyone else often has more strike outs as well!

Although we are talking about your first catalog here, it doesn't hurt to have the next catalog in mind while working on this one. A catalog is much like a train; once you get it started it has a momentum of its own. You just add new cars to it. If you start making plans now it will be much less work and less expense to produce your next catalog.

Here is an example of a simple change from one catalog to the next. Go back to Example 39. This page was based on three photos supplied by the manufacturer and a slide from the British Tourist Board. We sold out of the cape shown in the larger photo and were not able to get more of that item. The two items shown in the smaller photos had fair sales but less than expected. The manufacturer came up with a similar cape to replace the large one but he had no photo. He also found that the two smaller items sold slowly everywhere and he was stuck with a lot of backstock. The manufacturer offered us a much larger discount if we would run them again. We agreed.

For this catalog I wanted a new look, but I wanted to reuse what I could in order to keep expenses down. I used a model to show the new cape I was featuring and planned a photo of about the same size as the previous one. I wanted to show this new cape in two colors so I featured one on the model and had a little insert box featuring the second color: white.

I found a lovely pin that would replace the slide and dropped it into place. I left the old copy in with the old price for the smaller photos but added a slash for emphasis through the old prices and put a new line with the sale price below. The result is Example 45. We were able to save most of an old page and feature a new product for about 30% of the cost of an all new page. More importantly, this page went on to sell about 40% better than the original.

So now you are at the final stage. If you are stuck and don't know what to do with a page—just do something! If it's good it will grow and show you it's good. If it's bad it will look bad and you will start to fix it and you will get something better. If you do nothing, you will get nowhere! Everyone is most frustrated at this point. You don't see all the good you've done; rather you see what's weak or missing. It is difficult having to make final decisions when you don't really know which way to go. I hope it helps to know that almost everyone else feels the same at this point. You have a deadline breathing down your neck and you want to go back to bed and pull the covers over your head. Well, too bad! You chose to do this. If you wanted to go the safe way, you would be sitting at a desk in some government agency!

Do your best, then move on. You'll get better the next time and the time after that. It is time now to get pages pasted up and type set. You have completed an entire catalog. Your practice has already shown you a few hundred ways to make the next one better. You've gone to school, but this time you were paid to go. You are in the catalog business.

EXAMPLE 45

E. MOHAIR RUANA. Wear this rich, luxurious mohair as a Ruana (shawl), accent piece or use it as a throw on your couch or reading chair. 48" x 72".

#664586 Stripe	**$85.00**
#6645651 Solid White	**$85.00**
#6645652 Solid Red	**$85.00**
#6645653 Solid Black	**$85.00**

F. TAPESTRY SCARVES. Rich, textured, 9" x 72" scarves from Tapestry, Ireland. A great accent piece.

F1. #569434	**$19.95**
F2. #569435	**$19.95**

G. RED ROISIN. Lovely Irish wool in a more tailored coat with a detachable scarf. Made in Ireland.

#569523 Red	**$195.00**
#569524 White	**$195.00**

H. THISTLE BROOCH. This Sterling Silver thistle brooch is hallmarked in Edinburgh. A glorious accent piece worn on jacket, blouse or coat. Shown actual size.
#247259 - $95.00.

I. TAPESTRY IRELAND SWEATER JACKET. Once again a classic fabric is transformed into a very special look in this stylish jacket. Made in Ireland. Fully lined.
#569101 - $175.00.
CLOSE OUT SAVE 30% - $122.50.

J. HELENA JACKET. These bold colors and designs are an exciting departure from the more conventional Irish Tapestry featuring dolman sleeves, contrasting ribbed trim on collar and cuffs and two slash pockets. Made in Ireland. One size fits all.
#569151 - $175.00.
CLOSE OUT SAVE 40% - $105.00.

TO ORDER CALL TOLL FREE
1-800-638-0430

CHAPTER THIRTEEN

The Paste-Up

Now that everything is moving along, it's time to bring it all together, much like a cook tries to get all the elements of a dinner ready at the same time. You told your printer you would deliver the catalog to him on a certain date. You now have a deadline. You know when you will be mailing your catalog and you have talked to suppliers about making sure goods are on hand and properly stocked. Now you have painted yourself into a corner and it's about this time you start wondering if you are crazy.

You must now get the final drafts of your pages ready for delivery to the printer. There are several ways of doing this. You can employ someone to set your type and do your paste-up or you can use copy from your typewriter or computer, and do the paste-up yourself. You might also have someone set the type, then paste it up yourself.

Hire Someone?

If you hire the work out, you can spend a lot or a little. Ask your printer if he has an in-house paste-up service and how much they charge. Since printers are making their money on printing, they often have a very competitive price on paste-up. Search the yellow pages for typesetters and ask how much they charge for typesetting and paste-up. Once again they can be competitive since they are doing two jobs and you can save a little on each. It is also smart to ask the small multiservice copy companies in your town. In addition to making copies, many of these companies do some typesetting and paste-up. Whatever you do, you should leave plenty of time since you must proofread the typesetting, correct errors, proofread again, correct final errors (there are always errors), review paste-ups, correct errors and approve final paste-ups. This work is not very complex. It is very tedious and boring.

Another benefit of planning ahead and leaving lots of time at this stage is that you can use time as a negotiating tool for lower prices. Every printer, typesetter and graphics studio has busy times and slow times. They also have staff that get paid by the hour. They also deal with people who are always rushing. Everybody wants a job done yesterday. When they get a job that is not a rush and they know they can pull it out on a slow day when they have two or three employees sitting around without work to do, they are delighted. I have often used this knowledge to negotiate as much as 35% off an already quoted price of my typesetting and paste-up job.

Until very recently you had to have your copy set and then pasted up. Not very complex, but time consuming. Now a lot of copy can be arranged in pages by computer and the entire process is becoming cheaper and easier. I recently had a local copy company typeset and paste-up an eight-page newsletter for me and they charged $25 a page! I thought that was great. In the past I have paid in the range of $50 a page for paste-up. A few years ago, I would have pushed harder for you to do more of your own work, but computers are making it so much cheaper that I find you may be well advised to have someone else do it for you.

If you pay someone to do the typesetting and paste-up, you will deliver all your bags minus the roughs. They will start working and within a few days you should get your first proofs back. These need to be carefully reviewed for mistakes. There are always mistakes at this stage. Don't be upset when you find them; just correct them. You return the corrected pages and get a final set back. You keep checking until there are no mistakes.

Do It Yourself?

It's not difficult to do it yourself, just tedious. You have to prepare the pages so the printer can make a plate from them. If you need to supply specific instructions you write them on an overlay so that the printer knows what you want. When a printer makes a mistake on your work and the mistake is his fault, he will correct it at no charge. If the mistake occurs because your directions are incorrect or not clear, the printer will correct it, but you pay for the correction.

A few things may seem mysterious about paste-up. If you do decide to do the paste-up yourself, I urge you to buy a more detailed book on the topic. There are several titles available in art stores. The one I've used for the last eight years or so is *Complete Guide to Paste-Up* by Walter Graham, Dot Paste-Up Supply, Nebraska. I think I paid about $12 for this book of over 200 pages on technique.

A lot of what you need to know will come from your printer since he wants the work delivered to him in the correct form. In fact many printers will give you layout and grid paper for your design and paste-up. If they don't have it, most stationery supply stores will.

Planning paper is really great stuff when you know how to use it. It comes in a number of forms and sizes so that you can lay out one page or a spread of two pages at a time. What is most important is that it permits you to arrange copy from your typewriter or word processor into pages. This stuff intimidated me for years and when I finally figured it out, I was amazed how simple it was to use.

Printers measure in picas. Six picas equal one inch. The good news is that probably unbeknownst to you some familiar things are tied to pica measurements. A standard typewriter produces six lines to one inch. The depth of one line is one pica. If you have a computer, look at your printer directions and you will see that most are set up in picas or have an option to switch to pica. The grid planning paper mentioned in the last paragraph is set up in picas. For years I thought the grids were just for neatness and never knew what all the numbers at the top and sides meant. Example 46 is a typical sheet of planning paper. The lines are light blue which means they won't reproduce when you copy the page. The center point is O. Not only is it easy to lay out straight lines on this paper, but it is also easy to see how much space your type and headlines require.

The height of letters is measured in points. One pica = 12 points. Sounds confusing but it isn't. Look at the chart in Example 46. I have drawn the letter A in six different point sizes. The grid is divided into multiples of 6 picas, so that the 60-point A is the height of 5×12 points (1 pica = 12 points). If you go to a stationery store to buy Press Type to use for headlines you will see it comes in point sizes. If you want a normal headline above your copy, you might use 24-point type. If you want a really big headline, you might use a 48- or 60-point type. Purchase some grid paper, a few different sizes of Press Type and play with them a bit; you will be amazed how quickly you can make up a page.

Let me suggest something you will find very helpful. Find the largest stationery supply store in your area and poke around the graphics supply section. Look at the Press Type and layout grids and curved rulers and border art. There are hundreds of new products on the shelf that enable anyone to design and lay out a catalog or newsletter. Read directions. Get a feel for what tools are available to you. If you haven't gone through a graphics section in a few years you will be amazed at what they now have available. These products are designed to simplify planning, design, lay out and paste-up.

You can purchase a scale that will help you determine how many lines of copy will fit in a space. Nobody uses glue for photos and art anymore. The new glue sticks and wax sticks are a real joy to work with. They are handy and leave no mess. If you have the budget to get your work typeset and pasted-up, I believe that is a good place to spend your money. But, if your budget is really cut to the bone, purchase a few supplies to make laying out your catalog easier.

EXAMPLE 46

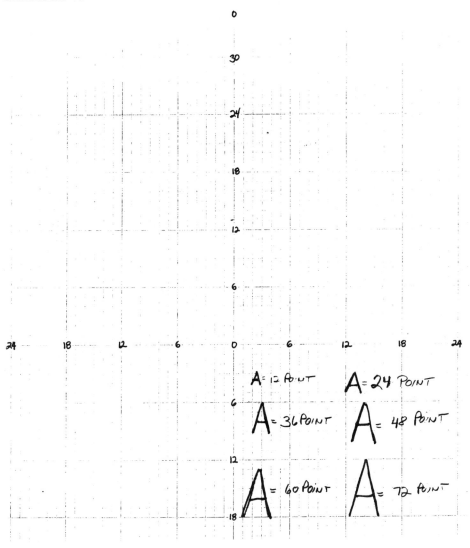

CHAPTER FOURTEEN

How Much Does it Cost?

Prices obviously will vary from place to place so the best I can do here is give you an average. I talked to a number of typesetters, graphics people and printers to get good estimates. All prices quoted are for the winter of 1990. For the purpose of a sample estimate, I have used a 32-page black and white catalog that is 8½" by 11".

Pre-Press Expenses

Pre-press includes all the costs incurred before your catalog goes to the printer. They are the costs of preparation and they are the costs you can control by the amount of work you do on your own.

COPY/LAYOUT/DESIGN: You know what you want to sell but you need to figure out what goes on which page, how the pages will look, what kind of headlines and type styles you'll use and the general organization of the entire catalog. You can hire a small agency to do this. You would give them the lists of products you want to sell and they would come up with a design. On the other hand you can do it yourself for as little as $50 in basic materials.

Hire a small agency	$ 1,600 to $ 3,200
Do it yourself	50 to 100
PHOTOGRAPHY:	
Hire a professional	$ 4,000 to $ 9,000
Do it yourself	500 to 1,000
(this includes cost of basic equipment)	
Some of both	$ 1,000 to $ 2,500
TYPESETTING	
Professional only	$ 500 to $ 1,000
PASTE-UP:	
Professional	$ 700 to $ 1,000
Do it yourself	100 to 300

TOTAL PRE-PRESS EXPENSES: If you send all the work out, you can easily spend over $14,000. If you cut every corner and do it all yourself you can do it for $1,100. Based on your skills and budget you can do it anywhere in between.

Printing and Mailing Costs

We used an estimate of 32 pages, printed on premium newsprint, bound and delivered to a mailing house. Prices can vary substantially based on the number printed but for our purposes we will say printing between 25,000 and 50,000 copies the cost should run in the range of $.23 to $.39 each. Additional examples for binding in order form are $.03 to $.05 each. List rental fees average about $.09 each, and postage and mail house fees average $.22 each.

How to Apply These Numbers to Your Project

You will notice that the pre-press expenses were quoted in total dollars. The cost to set up, photograph, lay out and paste-up the catalog is fixed. Let's say you spend $3,000 for pre-press. If you produce 1,000 catalogs your pre-press cost per catalog is $3; if you produce 30,000 catalogs the pre-press cost is $.10 per catalog. The cost per catalog changes as you adjust the number of catalogs printed, but the pre-press expense remains the same.

Printing costs are not fixed. All other things being the same, the cost per catalog is cheaper as you print more catalogs. In particular, the difference in cost is enormous when you compare a few thousand catalogs to tens of thousands. A quote on the various quantities for printing a 32-page, black and white catalog might be as follows.

Quantity	Total Cost	Cost per Catalog
1,000	$ 1,260	$ 1.26
2,000	1,680	.84
5,000	3,050	.61
10,000	4,400	.44
25,000	9,750	.39
50,000	11,500	.23
100,000	18,000	.18
200,000	34,000	.17

Let's start looking at these numbers in a variety of ways for a hypothetical catalog. Let us assume you have developed your own small mail list of 5,000 names and your pre-press expense is $3,000. You want to test the catalog business but you don't want to risk a lot of money. How much will it cost to produce and mail 1,000 catalogs? 2,000 catalogs? 5,000 catalogs?

For 1,000 catalogs you have $3,000 pre-press + $1,260 printing + $0.00 list rental (you have 5,000 names of your own) + $0.22 each for postage and mail fees ($220) or a total of $4,480; cost per catalog is $4.48.

For 2,000 catalogs you have $3,000 pre-press + $1,680 printing + $0.00 list rental (you have 5,000 names of your own) + 0.22 each for postage and mail fees ($440) or a total of $5,120; cost per catalog is $2.56.

For 5,000 catalogs you have $3,000 pre-press + $3,050 printing + $0.00 list rental (you have 5,000 names of your own) + $0.22 each for postage and mail fees ($1,100) or a total of $7,150; cost per catalog is $1.43. What happens if we jump the number of catalogs to 25,000? 50,000?

For 25,000 catalogs you have $3,000 pre-press + $9,750 printing + $1,800 list rental (your free 5,000 names + 20,000 names at $0.09 each) + $0.22 each for mail fees ($5,500) or a total of $20,050; cost per catalog is $0.80.

For 50,000 catalogs you have $3,000 pre-press + $11,500 printing + $4,050 list rental (your free 5,000 names + 45,000 names at $0.09 each) + $0.22 each for mail fees ($11,000) or a total of $29,550; cost per catalog is $0.59.

How Much Can I Make?

Once again we are dealing with a question that is almost impossible to answer. If you are selling sailboats in your catalog, you might have an average sale of $48,000. If you mail 1,000 catalogs and one person buys a boat you have a return of one-tenth of a percent and you make money. If you are selling bumper stickers at a dollar each and your average customer buys two for a total of $2 and 999 people buy from the 1,000 catalogs you mail, you lose money even though you have 99% return.

In the general gift and clothing industry, which seems to be one of the largest segments of the market, it seems a rate of return is considered good if it is in the range of 2% to 4%. Once again you must relate rate of return to the average sale. In the gift and clothing market average sales seem to run $45 to $85. These numbers come from an unscientific review of approximately 40 mail lists currently on the market. I have skipped the low end and high end and concentrated on the successful middle part of the market.

What is a 3% return with an average sale of $60? That means that 3% of the catalogs you mail will generate an order and the average order will be for $60.

QUESTION: If you mail 1,000 catalogs and get a 3% return with an average $60 order, how many orders will you get? What is the total income? What is your income per catalog? Using the example of cost per catalog for 1,000 at $4.48, how is your business doing so far? Answer the same questions for a mailing of 50,000 catalogs.

ANSWER: If 3% of 1,000 catalogs is 30 orders, and 30 × $60 (average order) is $1,800, then income per catalog ($1,800 total income divided by 1,000 catalogs mailed) is $1.80. That's lousy! Your cost per catalog is $4.48 and your income per catalog is $1.80. You lose!

If 3% of 50,000 catalogs is 1,500 orders, and 1,500 × $60 (average order) is $90,000, then income per catalog ($90,000 total income divided by 50,000 catalogs mailed) is $1.80. That's a little better. Your cost per catalog is $0.59 (see above) and your income per catalog is $1.80. You are still in the game!

I am telling you that two identical catalogs, with identical pre-press costs and identical rates of return and average sales can have completely different results based solely on the number of catalogs mailed. It is critical that you keep your cost per catalog down. At the same time you have a budget that limits your ability to produce large numbers of catalogs. I have often been approached by small business people ready to try a first catalog. In general, if they are looking at a first mailing under 10,000 catalogs, I suggest that they don't try it. Why? The cost per catalog is so high that success is unlikely.

Total Expenses

We have concentrated on the specific costs of the catalog but you must not forget that you have all the ordinary expenses of your business to account for before you see that magic number at the bottom of your profit and loss statement. I've reviewed a business plan for a sophisticated businessman who saw that his projected income per catalog was about $2.75 and his cost per catalog about $0.50. This gave him a $2.25 profit per catalog. He estimated his cost of goods sold at 45%, which means on every $2.75 sale his gross profit was $1.51 (55% of $2.75). He subtracted the $.50 cost per catalog and saw he made $1 profit on every catalog sold. He estimated a first mailing of 200,000 catalogs and thought he was going to pocket $200,000 in profit.

In his excitement he forgot that he also had to pay for rent, utilities, employees, supplies and the myriad other expenses involved in running his business. There are many books and forms available on basic bookkeeping that will explain the use of balance sheets and profit and loss statements. That is not the purpose of this book. My goal is to show you how to estimate expenses and income so that you can apply the results to your business plan. You can then plug your estimates into projected profit and loss statements in order to evaluate the potential success or failure of your planned business.

What you have now is a working method for putting a catalog together and estimating its cost and potential profitability. Hopefully, you know the difference between total costs and cost per catalog.

Hopefully, you understand the importance of testing different numbers so that you get a feel for the impact of change on your projections.
In any planning you do, you should have a few variations. What
happens if your sales are higher? Or lower? Where do you break even?
Most importantly, when you have a good sense of how numbers effect
each other, you tend to be better able to see how and where you can
decrease expenses and increase profits.

CHAPTER FIFTEEN

Increasing Profits

There are many ways you can use your catalog to increase your profits. Send a copy of your current catalog to potential new suppliers. Tell them you are interested in more information about their products. This is especially useful if you are featuring products by a direct competitor of that supplier. We had some suppliers that would not give us the time of day when we were small, but began to trip over themselves trying to please us as we grew. They hated seeing their arch rival featured in our catalog. Eventually they began to ask, "What does it take to get into your catalog?" The answer was always a better deal than we presently had.

Plan "sale" or "special" items for your catalog. They should not just happen. You should buy for this purpose so that you can maximize your profit.

Every "extra" item added to an order is highly profitable. Let us say a customer decides to buy two items from you for a cost of $40. The catalog cost and shipping cost are part of that sale. If you convince that customer to buy an extra item or two, your profit is much higher since the catalog cost and shipping have not changed.

A list of ways to get "extra" sales includes the following:

1) Combine items for specials. We increased our tweed tie sales by over 70% when we advertised "Buy three, take a fourth one free." Instead

of an average sale of $15, with a profit of $10, we had an average sale of $45, with a profit of $30. Always look for these combinations on high markup items.

2) Combine items that are not profitable enough on their own. We did this with food items that were not high market or high ticket but sold well in our shop. An inexpensive Irish cookbook that sold for $5 did not generate enough profit alone, but when it was sold with an Irish mug, selling for $6 into which we put a pack of ten Irish tea bags that sold for $.95, it worked. Each item was not profitable enough for the catalog alone, but as a unit it made for a fun $12 item and we sold a reasonable number.

3) When you take phone orders, you should always have a "daily phone special." After the order taker asks "Would you like to order anything else today?" and is given a "No," the reply can be something to the effect that "We have a daily special for customers ordering by phone. Today we are offering the new *Bagpipes for Christmas* album, which normally sells for $12.95, at $8.95. Would you like us to include one with your order?" You'll be amazed by the number of people that will say yes. All "extra" sales!

4) Knowledgeable employees on the phone know to suggest additional purchases from the catalog. If someone orders golf balls, "Do you need any tees to go with them?" should be the response. When people order shoes, ask if they need shoe trees or some new socks. I believe customers appreciate a good salesperson checking on the completeness of an order without being too pushy. Each small increase is profit that will make your business a success.

5) Advertise pre-release specials. A note to the effect that you will be featuring certain items at a later date but are willing to give an "early bird" special of a percentage off is a great way of selling items you don't even stock! We did this with tweed jackets, giving a 25% discount if the customer ordered before we placed our fall orders. It also let us fill odd sizes we might not add to the normal order.

6) Consider taking special orders and custom orders. Once again you can get paid before you stock an item which limits your risk and investment in inventory. It also allows you to offer a range of services not usually available in larger catalogs and companies. The down side is that special orders usually take a lot more work and generate a lot of headaches.

Ask for customer referrals. We always include a space for listing names of people that might like to receive our catalog. It is a source for thousands of new names per year that have a very high buying rate from us. We treated these referral names like gold. Make sure you ask!

Read and keep learning about mail order. Get on lists for trade publications and read books that may apply to you. After you hear the advice of the new experts, use your own best judgment. Some things that work for most people are not going to work for your niche of the market and vice versa. But you should keep abreast of what others are doing and thinking.

Break a rule on occasion. You are where you are because you relied on yourself and trusted your instincts. Sometimes instinctual behavior is the right way to go. I never sold very many bagpipes in my shop; nevertheless, I wanted to feature them in our catalog. I did not expect to sell many. The rule I would violate is the one about items justifying their space in the catalog. I was going to put something in that would probably cost more in space than it would make. I wanted to do it anyway because I wanted people to say, "Gee! Look at this. They even have bagpipes!" I felt it would make us look different and authentic since no other catalogs featured pipes.

As it turned out we started selling bagpipes like crazy and they became one of the most reliable sellers over the years. We had a big hit for all the wrong reasons. Thank God I listened to my instincts!

Rent or swap space in your catalog. We were approached at different times by people selling items we were not interested in pursuing. Our market was so specialized that they wanted to advertise with us so we figured out a rate and if the product was compatible, allowed them to advertise. Some examples of compatible offers were travel plans to Great Britain, Scotland and Ireland, or home delivery of Scottish salmon and cheeses. These swaps or rentals were usually pure profit for us and our customers enjoyed receiving them.

Remember that the box going out to your customer is very valuable. "Someone who just bought is most likely to buy something again?" We would insert offers from other companies into our boxes for a fee as long as the offers were compatible. A flyer on air fares or vacations in Great Britain would be typical. We had some on British coins, food items, magazines and book clubs. We received the flyers from the advertiser and charged an average of $0.15 for each one we inserted in a shipping box. We would sometimes have five inserts per box, which meant $0.75 extra on every box going out. Once again, this was pure profit!

Make inquiries about inserting your catalog or flyer in someone else's box. If you are aware of someone else selling compatible products you should ask to rent space from them or swap space. This is a great way to prospect for new customers and much less expensive than mailing.

Make sure you enclose a current copy of your catalog with the order going out to the customer. If the customer is pleased with his shipment it is very likely he will turn around and order again as long as you make it easy for him. Give him a new order form, etc.

Ask your suppliers for exclusives. You only need some variation on a product for it to be uniquely your own. A slightly different design in jewelry or fabric or an added feature lets you have your own item. Customers like exclusives.

Don't be afraid to develop your own products. We had a very difficult time getting appropriate Christmas cards with a Scottish or Irish theme. We ended up designing our own and having a local printer make them for us. It turned out to be very profitable and we even sold the cards wholesale to other Irish and Scottish shops that also had the same problem locating something appropriate.

An entire side business developed for us because we wanted to sell practice chanters. The practice chanter is the instrument on which one learns to play the bagpipe. It is usually made of wood and roughly a foot long and looks something like a recorder. Also, the few books available at the time all required a teacher. We believed an inexpensive self-teaching book would enable us to sell more of these practice chanters since America is a real "do-it-yourself" kind of place. We talked a bagpipe teacher friend into writing a book which we produced ourselves and published much like a small catalog.

The book increased our sale of practice chanters about ten-fold and in response to requests led us to produce a companion cassette to go with the book. We then had a box made into which we placed a book, cassette and practice chanter and labeled it our "Teach Yourself the

Bagpipe Kit." This was an item that retailed at $40 and we sold thousands of them year after year.

This led us to having many products made to our design over the years, from custom sweaters to our own Pipe Majors tea. There are many companies that cater to private label work for catalogs and there is now a private label show held annually in New York for the clothing trade.

Collectors Clubs and Newsletters

One of the most innovative things we did merits some explaining. In order to reach our best customers more frequently we developed a club newsletter. I was worried about the cost of creating and mailing such a small circulation item of only four pages; consequently, I created a collectors club. The club was meant to let us list items that may not have been suitable for the regular catalog or that had limited availability. I advertised the club with announcements in the catalog and placed flyers in the boxes of merchandise sent to our customers. I used a series of cutouts pasted on a page around an announcement for an eye catching but inexpensive ad as shown in Example 47.

For the $10 fee members received four newsletters. In other words we had a budget of $2.50 per copy to create a newsletter! The newsletters were four pages and measured 8½" × 11." I wrote the copy and did the photography myself. I had the layout, typesetting and paste-up done at a local small press. They did it by computer and charged $125 for the entire job! A normal print run would be approximately 1,400 copies and the cost of printing ran about $0.37 each.

All four pages of a newsletter are shown in Examples 48–51. You can see that they are straightforward and simple to set up. We made money on the newsletter before we sold anything because I overestimated the cost of producing it. I have recommended to one or two of my clients that were very limited on funds and wanted to start very small that they use this format for a first catalog. Think about it.

If you were going to start very small and mail only 2,000 catalogs, you could use this format and do the entire project of layout, printing and mailing for around $1,500. Interesting isn't it? Remember that you don't have 32 pages of product but this might work for a first step

EXAMPLE 47

COLLECTORS CLUB

In our travels we come across many unusual items. We find old advertising signs, prints, memorabilia and antiques of Scottish or Irish interest. We often meet small craftsmen who make only a few items each year. It seems we constantly find "one-of-a-kind" or limited edition items.

On our buying trips we always watch for manufacturers that are closing shop or going out of business. We sometimes buy out the entire inventory of these companys. This may leave us buying 400 bagpipe cases here and 700 blue Angora sweaters there, all at a huge discount.

In Mail Order it is not financially practical to feature items that are one-of-a-kind or in limited production. Yet we would like to share these "collectables" and "specials" with you, our mail order buyers.

Starting in January 1987, we will produce a Newsletter featuring all our "Specials", Antiques, Memorabilia and "Sale" items. These Newsletters will be produced separately from our catalog. We now mail over 500,000 catalogs; however, the Newsletter will only be mailed by subscription to members of the Collectors Club.

We will mail at least two Newsletters each year and we will mail when we have a good collection to offer you. All Newsletters will be mailed on the same day, giving all club members an equal chance at one-of-a-kind items. Membership is $10.00 per year. The first Newsletter will be mailed in late January 1987 and membership must be reserved by December 20th, 1986 in order to receive this 1st edition.

Collectors Club 1987 $10.00

when your product selection and funds are limited. Another variation would be to keep the mailing small as you grow and charge a small amount for the newsletter. Instead of $10 a year, make it $3 or $5.

I think it's a mistake to charge for a catalog if you are appealing to a general audience. If you are unique in what you do and hitting a very specialized audience then some sort of fee may be reasonable. The best is to do both as I did. Either way, the newsletter merits some serious examination. Once again, I do not offer my newsletter as an example of great design. I include it here as a good working example of what an ordinary person can do in order to get his foot in the door of mail order.

Product Codes

Codes should not be a bunch of numbers with no meaning. Properly established, codes can help you organize items and prevent many mistakes from occurring. People have poor hand writing or bad eye-sight and often make little mistakes in orders that cause the wrong items to be delivered to them. It is very expensive to return and replace items besides which it annoys your customer. Our coding system was quite elaborate so I will outline only its basic details.

All products were categorized into one of ten classifications from 0 to 9. The first digit of the code reflected that classification.

0—records, tapes	3—music
1—gift items	4—books
2—jewelry	5—clothing, etc.

As a first line of defense our pullers and our shippers knew that if they picked up an item going out that was a piece of jewelry and its code didn't start with 2 then something was wrong.

Based on the first digit classification we had codes for sizes, colors and styles. For example under our clothing classification we had ten categories.

0—blouses	3—capes
1—aran sweaters	4—coats
2—fashion sweaters	5—skirts

The third digit in the code was color:

0—not applicable	3—white

EXAMPLE 48

SCOTTISH & IRISH IMPORTS LTD.
PIPER

| Vol. 1 No. 1 | 197 MAIN STREET | ANNAPOLIS, MD | 21401 | MARCH 1987 |

THE COLLECTORS CLUB

The PIPER is published on a highly erratic schedule and is the official newsletter of the *SCOTTISH & IRISH IMPORTS LTD COLLECTORS CLUB.* In this issue you will find a cross section of items. Many are one of a kind, some are new items being shown for the first time and some are special close out sales. We have already purchased many more antique and collectable items, but they are being collected in containers for shipment so you'll see them in the next newsletter.

All newsletters are mailed on the same day. If you see an item marked *"one of a kind"*. or *"limited supply"*, we suggest that you order immediately. All special prices and special offers in this newsletter end March 30, 1987.

PUB MIRROR - This one is approximately 23" X 30", it's an advertisment for Colman's mustard and features a color portrait of King George V.
Only one available   199010 .. $45.00

SMALL MIRROR - An exact copy of the Pub Mirror above only this one is 10" x 13".
Only one available   199011 .. $15.00

ORIGINAL SPORRAN FLASK - Originally designed to fit in sporrans, this elegant flask will fit unobtrusively into any jacket pocket. Holds almost a quarter pint.   19401 .... $35.00

HIGHLAND CLANS & TARTANS - by R. W. Munro, Originally published in 1977 this beautiful book contains over 150 full color and black and white illustrations, out of print for the last 6 or 7 years. Excellent Value!   4239213 .... $6.95

THISTLE TANKARD - Beautiful silver plate tankard in typical 18th century fluted design. A new product. Highly embossed thistle handle.
               146012 .... $45.00

QUAICH - The traditional two handed drinking vessel of Scotland. This silver plated version is 8" long with intricate celtic designs on the handles.
               146010 .... $24.95

OLD SODA WATER BOTTLE - Doesn't work but looks attractive in kitchen or bar. Heavy cut glass, reads "G & P Barrie Ltd.", "Glasglow & Dundee"
               199003 .... $25.00

THISTLE MUG - This one pint silver plated mug has an embossed thistle handle and slightly flared sides. Just arrived at the shop.   146011 .... $29.95

ROYAL HERITAGE - Over 360 pages filled with black & white and color photos of Britain's Royal Builders and Collectors. Originally $25.00.
               486091 .... $14.95

EXAMPLE 49

CIGARETTE PICTURE CARDS

I remember collecting football (British not American) cards from the back of Typhoo tea boxes as a boy. Since most people in my family drank McGrath's or Shamrock tea, I was forced to poke through the neighbor's garbage—an occupation that infuriated my mother.

Way before American baseball cards, beautiful, full color cards were found on British cigarettes. The tobacco companies often sold collection books for a penny or two and you tried to fill them all in. These days those old books of cigarette cards are becoming valuable collectables in their own right. The few we list here make wonderful mementos.

199004 Book of Cigarette Cards — "Military Uniforms of the British Empire Overseas" issued by John Player & Sons 1938.
All 50 cards complete $25.00

199005 Cigarette Album - Gilbert & Sullivan 2nd series, Players, full set of 50 -issued late 1930's, I think! $25.00

199006 Cigarette Album - History of British Empire, Churchmans Cigarette Co., April 1934
Only 7 cards filled in $5.00

199007 Set of 36 cards out of serries of 50, fair to poor condition, Badges of the R.A.F. - November 1937.
No book, just cards $5.00

199008 Empire in Arms - 1917, An account of the British Army, Navy and Colonial forces in World War I. Approximately 350 pages with some early photographs and illustrations, slight water damage, very interesting book, very patriotic, day to day organization information.
1 copy $25.00

199009 Story of 25 Eventful Years in Pictures. Over 500 pages of photos of Great Britain from 1910 to 1935 - Fascinating book.
1 copy $25.00

BAGPIPE WALKING STICK

We have two prototypes of a handcrafted blackwood walking stick that cleverly unscrew to become a practice chanter. Manufactured by Grainger & Campbell. The photo shows Jim playing the chanter middle sections. Assembled length approximately 38".
3201 . . . . $145.00

199002 D.J. McCallum's Perfection Scotch Whisky. Old advertising flask is glass with a nickel silver base and leather top. Screw cap - still able to be used. Approximately 6" high, holds about 1 pint.
. . . . $45.00

199001 Edinburgh Savingsk Bank. These were given to children to save up their change. When full you brought the little bank to the Big Bank where they had the key and deposited the coins to your account. Although not given out anymore, Edinburgh Banks still have keys to open these little mementos. Metal, Approximately 4" x 4" $20.00

EXAMPLE 50

STONEWARE CROCK - Approximately 6" high by 8" wide, on side marked 6 lb., Front reads "Malcolm Buchanan Grocer & Wine Merchant, Rothesay.
199012 .... $25.00

BUCHAN POTTERY WHISKEY JUGS: - Buchnan Pottery makers of Thistle Pottery, also make special promotional jugs for various distillers. We have a small selection for you odd people who collect them. All are in good shape and all are empty.

    199013 Tuxedo Old Scotch Whiskey $6.00
    199014 Grants Deluxe Scotch $6.00
    199015 Glenfiddich Master Crock $6.00
    199016 House of Peers "Old Reserve" $6.00
    199017 Wm. Maxwell Deluxe $6.00
    199018 Burns Cottage $6.00

LAST MINUTE SPECIALS

BLANKET CAPE - Shown in last 3 catalogs. Available in Black Watch, Dress Gordon or Royal Stewart. While they last!!!
57 .... Were $69.95......Close out $49.95

SCOTTISH ARMS MAKERS - Book by Charles Whitelaw, a dictionary of makers of Firearms, Edged weapons and Armor Working in Scotland from 15th Century to 1870. A standard reference — My old copy cost about $45.   CLOSE OUT— 340 pages.
19952 .... SPECIAL $4.95

IRISH FARMHOUSE CLOCK - Made entirely of wood, runs on gravity. This is a classic beauty, overall length 50", Dial diameter 12¼". Only 3 left!
999 .... Was $395.......CLOSE OUT $195.

HAND ENAMELED ONE SHILLING COIN - on 18" chain - 1963 Shilling in white, red, blue and gold.
Quite Distinctive! !
2324 .... Was $25.......CLOSE OUT $14.95

HUNTING PRINT - by Sir Edwin Landseer. This full color, limited edition print, is museum quality, beautifully trimmed with a tweed border under glass. Approximately 34" x 28". Only one available.
199042 .... $350.

BOTHY WORKSHOP

HANDMADE EGG CUP, beautifully turned from one piece of walnut. Made by Duncan Harley of Aberdeen.
A work of Art...
104102 .... $75.00

WOOD TOP & HOLDER by Bothy, Draw string bag, great toy!!
104101 .... $9.95

WOOD CUP AND BALL TOSS GAME - from Bothy Workshop, comes with little bag.
104103 .... $9.95

EXAMPLE 51

CLOSE OUT SALE

MANS KILT SHIRT—As advertised in our regular catalog, these Linen-cotton blend shirts are available in small, medium or large.

77 KILT SHIRT.......... WAS $45.00 FINAL SALE $29.95

	WAS	FINAL SALE
RECORDS AND CASSETTES	$8.95	$4.95
05026 SCOTTISH ACCORDIAN HITS	$8.95	$4.95
05075 SCOTTISH ACCORDIAN HITS VOL.2	$8.95	$4.95
05038 CALEDONIA PIPE BAND	$8.95	$4.95
05116 BEST SCOTTISH DANCE BANDS	$8.95	$4.95
05027 TARTAN LADS —by THE LOIHSIDE	$8.95	$4.95
06004 ALEXANDER BROS. - OLD FRIENDS DO	$8.95	$4.95
058 EDINBURGH TATOO 1983	$8.95	$4.95

GOODRICH & CO. GOLF SIGN -(shown in our last catalog page 8) 18" x 30", hand painted with a three-dimensional golfer and four early golf balls. Only one available!

182003 .... WAS $450.00...... SALE $250.00

DEFECTIVE BAGPIPES - These pipes have all their parts, but for some reason or other don't play - Usually a defective bag. They do, however make great wall hangings. While they last.

199304 .... $25.00

KIT - Our original teach yourself the bagpipe kit is being replaced by a new kit; consequently, we are closing out the old kits. They were $49.95 and we will sell them for $29.95 until they are gone.

199359 .... $29.95

197 Main Street
Annapolis, Maryland 21401
(301) 267-7094

1—red   4—blue
2—black   5—green

The fourth and fifth digits were for the size when appropriate or 00 when not appropriate.

Using this information, the code for a red Aran sweater, size 40 was 5 (clothing), 1 (Aran sweater), 1 (red), 40 (size). When shipping had a sweater to go out they matched the codes with the item description as a double check to make sure we were shipping the correct product. The system should be refined to your specific needs.

Basic business principles apply to all businesses and you can learn a lot studying business in general. In all forecasting for my business I found it helpful to overestimate expenses and underestimate income. That way I was rarely caught short. I am still amazed at the number of new companies that do the opposite. It seems they must be unpleasantly surprised on a regular basis!

You must have a good working idea about the numbers and profitability of your business but you must also be wary of too much bookkeeping. It is sometimes tempting to prepare so many reports and break downs of sales and expenses that you spend all your time examining reports rather than making decisions or selling.

Mail order is a business. It has its strengths as well as its shortcomings just like any other business. It is not a way to get rich quick with a minimal amount of work. Some fortunes are made and some are lost.

It does allow for self management. Some people think that working 60 hours a week for yourself is far superior to working 40 hours a week for someone else. I must admit to being one of those people.

Mail order can be a great way to expand your business without moving or opening a branch. There are many difficulties in opening a second shop, the greatest being finding a manager and staff that you can rely on. If your manager quits in the second shop that is two hundred miles away, what do you do? Commute?

Growth is not always the answer in business. Sometimes you can develop an operation to a size where you can run it with a few other people and make a nice profit. How I wish I knew when to stop. Growth led me to more money and more headaches. I ended up doing many things I hated doing and giving up the parts of the business I thought I was good at. I watched sales soar along with hours worked and headaches only to find that the bottom line net profit had not really changed that much.

I like mail order. It allows us to operate from anywhere; we don't have to be in the mall or on Main Street. We can control our working environment a lot more. It is a challenging and constantly changing business. It is a good start up or a side business when you are trying to move from one career to another. It can be as simple or elaborate as you wish to make it.

I wanted to give you a straight forward and honest picture of what's involved in putting your first catalog together. I hope you have a better sense of what to expect. If I helped you decide that mail order is not for you, then I'm glad I saved you some time and money. If I encouraged you to feel that you want to give mail order a shot, then I'm glad that I was able to help you move forward.

CHAPTER SIXTEEN

Evaluating Your Catalog

Congratulations! You got your first catalog out. The second one is a lot easier and cheaper to produce. Much of the expense and set up for the first catalog does not have to be done again. If you bought a camera you don't need another. Some of your layouts will not change at all. Some will change only a little. Many items will not need new photos or drawings. Most importantly you learned a lot by doing the first one and you are now ready to improve.

All of your marketing decisions on the first catalog were guess work. You guessed at what might sell. You guessed at the average sale. You guessed at the number of orders you might receive. It was frightening having to guess at so many important things with so little information.

By tracking all sales from your catalog you have a powerful tool for projecting future sales and returns. This kind of information should make each catalog more efficient and more profitable. If you sell 200 copies of a certain kind of book you will likely sell 200 copies of a similar new book, assuming that you mail the same number of catalogs. If you double the number of catalogs, you might anticipate selling 400 copies. You should get a better idea about what types of things your customer buys. You will slowly develop an eye for "My customer will buy both of these things, but they will buy three times as many of these."

Open a catalog and write down the number of units sold and the total income for each item. Do it right on the page with a marker or

EXAMPLE 52

pen. Then add up the total dollar sales for that page and write it down also. A page might look like this.

Of the six items on this page, two were given a large display and the other four were given half as much space. The entire page generated $4,000 in sales. Item A has 25% of the display space and it generated 24% of the sales ($960 divided by $4,000). That seems just about perfect.

Items B and C both had strong sales and are close in value. Together, they take up 25% of the display space, but they account for $1,490 ($710 + $780) or 37% of the sales. Excellent. They should probably have more space to see if they will do even better. It would be acceptable to leave them unchanged. They are doing well as they are and percentage of sales are not way beyond the space they occupy.

Item D has 25% of the display space and accounts for 3% of the sales. Big loser! Yank it! But try to figure out why it was a loser so you don't repeat that mistake again.

Item E accounted for 34% of total sales yet it took up only 12½% of the display space! This is the best selling item on the page and it definitely deserves more space. I'd probably assign it the space that D had at a minimum. It might deserve even more space. Item F is a big loser. Try to figure out why it did so poorly then dump it.

What might you do to improve the performance of this page in your next catalog? One quick solution might be to keep A, B, and C just the way they are. Reshoot item E and put it where D was and try two new items where E and F were. There are a lot of other possibilities.

Let's say that you got these results from a mailing of 25,000 catalogs. You were happy with the returns and you decide that you will mail 75,000 catalogs the next time. About how many units of Item B do you think you might sell? What are your projected sales for this page? Hopefully you said approximately 108 items and $12,000 + (three times the original numbers). Isn't it nice having a more accurate gauge for estimating.

Another way to use numbers is less obvious. You should have a good idea about how many boxes you can pack and ship in a day. If you have one employee that can pack and ship 100 boxes a day and you figure you get 500 orders a week you are just fine. If you triple the mailing and expect an additional 200 orders a day you are going to need two more employees. Not one, not three. You can use the rates to project the employees you may need.

The best season for most catalogers is Christmas. Sales boom from September through December. You plan to mail 100,000 catalogs for the Christmas season and you generally get a 4% return on mailings (4,000 orders). You can use the rates to plan your mail drop so that you get a fairly smooth flow of orders over the season rather than mailing 50,000 catalogs in September and 50,000 in December. A smooth flow of orders means one employee could handle all the orders over the 16-week period rather than two or three employees needed for two spurts with a gap in between.

A careful review of sales can help in every aspect of your business planning from inventory control to ordering the proper number of shipping cartons in the correct sizes. Mail order is very much a business of buying patterns and statistics. A good selling item will often sell well for a long period of time. Other items are seasonal or short lived hits. You will develop a sense about which is which over time. You will develop patterns. You will know your customer buys one type of book and not another. Careful interpretation of previous buying patterns will enable you to predict future buying patterns with remarkable accuracy. It's in the numbers but you have to look for it.

Sources & Resources

TRADE ORGANIZATIONS

THE DIRECT MARKETING ASSOCIATION
11 West 42nd Street
New York, NY 10036
(212) 768-7277
This association has books, periodicals, tapes, seminars, and sources
for just about anything you want to know about mail order.

TRADE PUBLICATIONS

DM NEWS
19 W. 21st Street
New York, NY 10010
Published every Monday; distributed free of charge to qualified U.S.
direct marketers and their agencies. Cost for nonqualified subscribers
is $75. in U.S., more for Canada and Europe.

DIRECT, CATALOG AGE, CATALOG PRODUCT NEWS
Hanson Publishing Group Inc.
Box 4949
Stamford, CT 06907
All three publications are sent without cost to senior executives in the
catalog industry; paid subscriptions are accepted for those not meeting
free circulation requirements for approximately $64 for each publica-
tion in the U.S., more in Canada, Mexico and Europe. Subscription
includes an annual copy of *The Sourcebook,* which lists professionals in
many phases of the catalog industry.

PRINTERS OF CATALOGS

ALDEN PRESS
2000 Arthur Avenue
Elk Grove Village, IL 60007
(708) 640-6000

FRY COMMUNICATIONS
800 West Church Road
Mechanicsburg, PA 17055
(800) 334-1429

GULF PRINTING
2210 West Dallas
Houston, TX 77019
(800) 423-9537

INTELLIGENCER PRINTING COMPANY
330 Eden Road
Lancaster, PA 17601
(717) 291-3100

JUDDS INCORPORATED
1500 Eckington Place N.E.
Washington, D.C. 20002
(202) 635-1200

NOLL PRINTING COMPANIES
100 Noll Plaza
Huntington, IN 46750
(800) 348-2886

PERLMUTER PRINTING COMPANY
4437 E. 49th Street
Cleveland, OH 44125
(800) 634-1262

PERRY PRINTING
575 West Madison Street
Waterloo, WI 53594
(414) 478-3551

QUAD/GRAPHICS
Pewaukee, WI 53072
(414) 691-9200

RINGIER AMERICA
One Pierce Place
Itasca, IL 60143
(708) 941-6000

JOHN ROBERTS COMPANY
9687 East River Road
Minneapolis, MN 55433
(612) 755-5500.

SPENSER PRESS INC.
90 Industrial Park Road
Hingham, MA 02043
(617) 749-5000

PRINTERS OF ORDER FORMS

B & W PRESS
41 Popes Lane
Danvers, MA 01923
(617) 595-4271

CONVERTAGRAPHICS
7702 Plantation Road NW
Roanoke, VA 24019
(703) 363-3346

MAIL-WELL GRAPHICS
P. O. Box 23600
Phoenix, AZ 85063
(800) 321-7267

WEBCRAFT TECHNOLOGIES
Route 1 and Adams Station
North Brunswick, NJ 08902
(201) 821-3796

LIST BROKERS AND MANAGERS

AMERICAN LIST COUNSEL
88 Orchard Road
Princeton, NJ 08543
(800) 252-5478

AZ MARKETING SERVICES
31 River Road
Cos Cob, CT 06807
(203) 629-8088

DIRECT MEDIA GROUP
220 Grace Church Street
Port Chester, NY 10573
(914) 937-5600

THE KLEID COMPANY, INC.
530 Fifth Avenue
New York, NY 10036
(212) 719-9788

MILLARD GROUP, INC.
10 Vose Farm Road
Peterborough, NH 03458
(603) 924-9262

RUBIN RESPONSE SERVICES
1111 Plaza Drive
Schaumburg, IL 60173
(708) 619-9800

WALTER KARL COMPANIES
135 Bedford Road
Armonk, NY 10504
(800) 527-5669

WOODRUFF-STEVENS ASSOCIATES
345 Park Avenue South
New York, NY 10010
(212) 685-4600

Index

address correction, 55
advertising flyers, 18
art, 19, 20, 35, 65-70; screening, 20; separating, 20
art director, 67
average sale, 96

backup products, 69, 79, 85
bid packets, 88
binding, 89
bulk mail permit, 53, 101

cameras, 68, 69
catalog evaluation, 135-138
catalog types: book, 19, 20, 21; electronics, 19; fashion, 19; jewelry, 19; records, 22; special interest, 19; technical, 19; cheshire labels, 53, 101; clip art, 38, 66; clip files, 18-19, 51
codes: customer, 98-99; mail lists, 96-98; merchandise, 127, 132
collectors club, 125
color, 51
column size, 22
competitors, 12, 13-14
computers, 33, 51, 97
copy, 19, 22, 71-73
cost per book, 98, 118, 119
covers: back, 18, 33, 53-56; color, 51; cover art, 38; design, 38; front, 18, 33, 37-52
"current occupant", 53
customer profile, 14, 15, 30, 31
customer referrals, 123

design, 17-26
direct marketing association, 96, 139

editing, 85
exclusives, 29, 123

file system, 75
final draft, 103-108
first rough, 32

grids, 78

Hollan bag system, 75

income per book, 97, 118
indicia, 53
inventory, 28, 33

labels, 53, 101
layout, 19, 20-26, asymmetrical, 20; four column, 20 21; symmetrical 20; sub heads 22; two column, 22; three column, 22
list brokers, 93-96
list codes, 96-97
list manager, 94
list selects, 94
logo, 38, 51
loss leaders, 29, 31

mail house, 100-101
mail lists, 93-99
manufacturer: negotiations, 29, 65, 121; source for art, 65
models, 20, 67

net profit, 119
newsletters, 125, 127

order forms, 19, 33, 57-64

page analysis, 77, 135, 136
page sales analysis, 77, 78
paste up, 109-119
peel off labels, 53, 100-101
phone orders, 122, 123
photography, 19, 20, 65-69; art direction, 67; do it yourself, 68-69; professional 66-67, references, 66; fees and services, 65, 66; ownership of negatives, 66; negotiations, 65; supplier, 82
picas, 111, 112
points, 112
postage 53, 100
pre press expenses 115, 116
preliminary questionnaire, 12
presstype, 112
pricing 28, 31
printers, 60, 87-92
print costs, 116-118
product benefit, 71, 72
product codes, 22
product development, 124, 125
product selection, 22, 24, 28, 29, 30, 31, 79; exclusives, 29; image 29; loss leaders, 29, 31; organization, 30; product list; 28, 30, 79; sale items, 29; combining items, 29
props, 67

Quarto, 32

rate of return, 96, 118
return envelopes, 57
return postage, 55
reverse, 87-88
roughs: first, 32-36; outline, 30, 32; second, 75

sale items, 121
sales projections, 118, 137
shipping inserts, 124
silhouettes, 87
size—for catalog, 33
sources, 139-143
space: justifying by sales, 29
specials, 121, 122; add on specials, 122; pre release specials, 122
special orders, 123
square inch analysis, 77, 135, 137
standard formats, 37

type size, 22
typographers, 110, 111